遇见中国

CHINA

卜力眼中的东方世界

[英] 亨利·阿瑟·卜力／著
[英] 莫蒂默·曼培斯／绘
李菲／译

上海社会科学院出版社

作者介绍

亨利·阿瑟·卜力
Henry Arthur Blake
（1840.1.8—1918.2.13）

英国派驻香港的第十二任总督（任期1898年11月25日—1903年7月29日）。他认识李鸿章、张之洞、郭嵩焘等一批晚清的重要人物。根据他在书中的陈述，他曾经到过中国南方的不少地区，最深入的是湖北武汉及四川等地。卜力任内也进行了不少建设，包括铺设电车轨道（1904年通车）、主持最高法院奠基礼（于1912年启用）。天星小轮、先施百货、《南华早报》也于卜力任内创立。

绘者介绍

莫蒂默·曼培斯
Mortimer Menpes
（1855.2.22—1938.4.1）

英国水彩画家，以人物肖像和民俗风景画著称，曾在英国伦敦皇家艺术学院学习过，毕业后成为插图师。他成名之后也曾编著过一些文化艺术丛书，其中最出名的就是曼培斯—科朗文化系列。他为这套丛书的每一部都画了插图，其中有不少是彩色的。根据曼培斯本人的日记和他女儿的回忆，他曾在中国、日本等东亚地区旅游与居住过一段时间，他的插图画的都是他自己的见闻经历。

译者介绍

李 菲

毕业于湖南师范大学外国语学院。译作有：《力量源自内心》《饥馑湖》《喜剧演员》《查理十二世的人马》《你一定爱读的极简世界史》《父与子（中英双语彩色全新版）》《德古拉》《极限控制》《数字解读世界史》《意大利的黄昏》《美国手记》等。

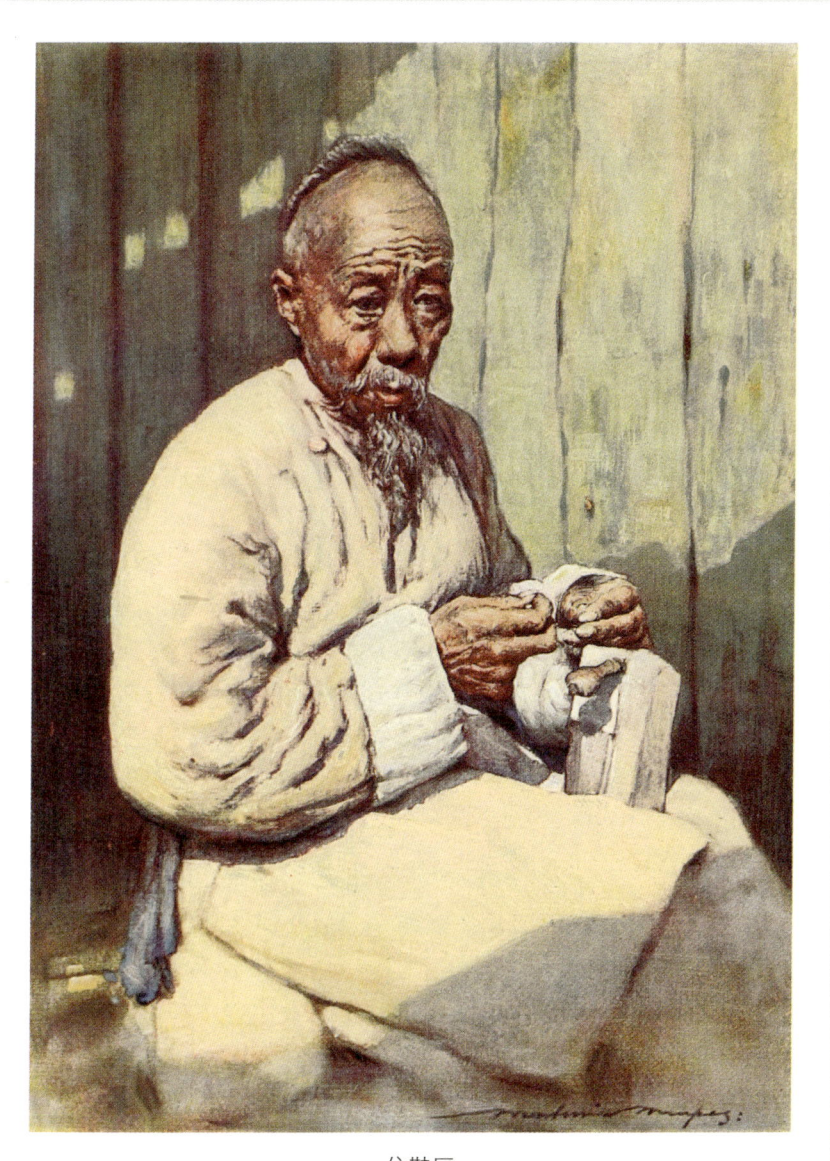

一位鞋匠

一条平静的运河

一个学生

舢板船

筷子

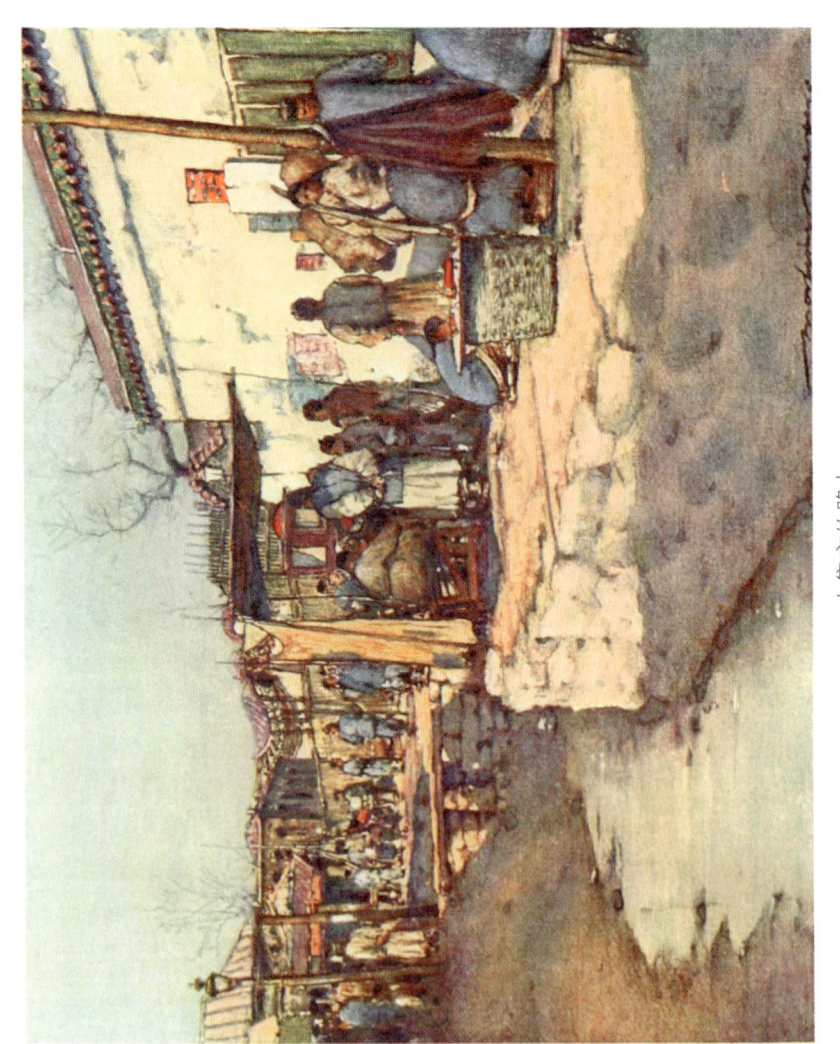

去集市的路上

一位祖父

避暑別墅

安静的跳棋游戏

等待顾客

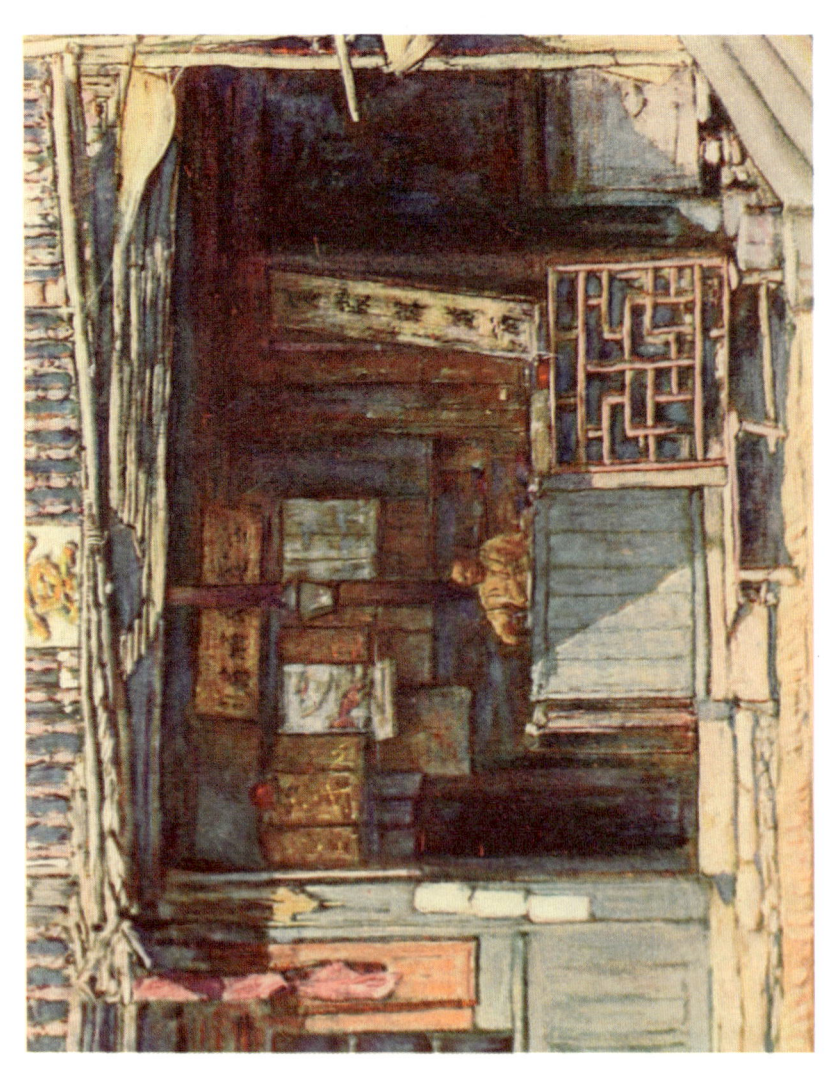

一位中国女孩

日暮中的平底帆船

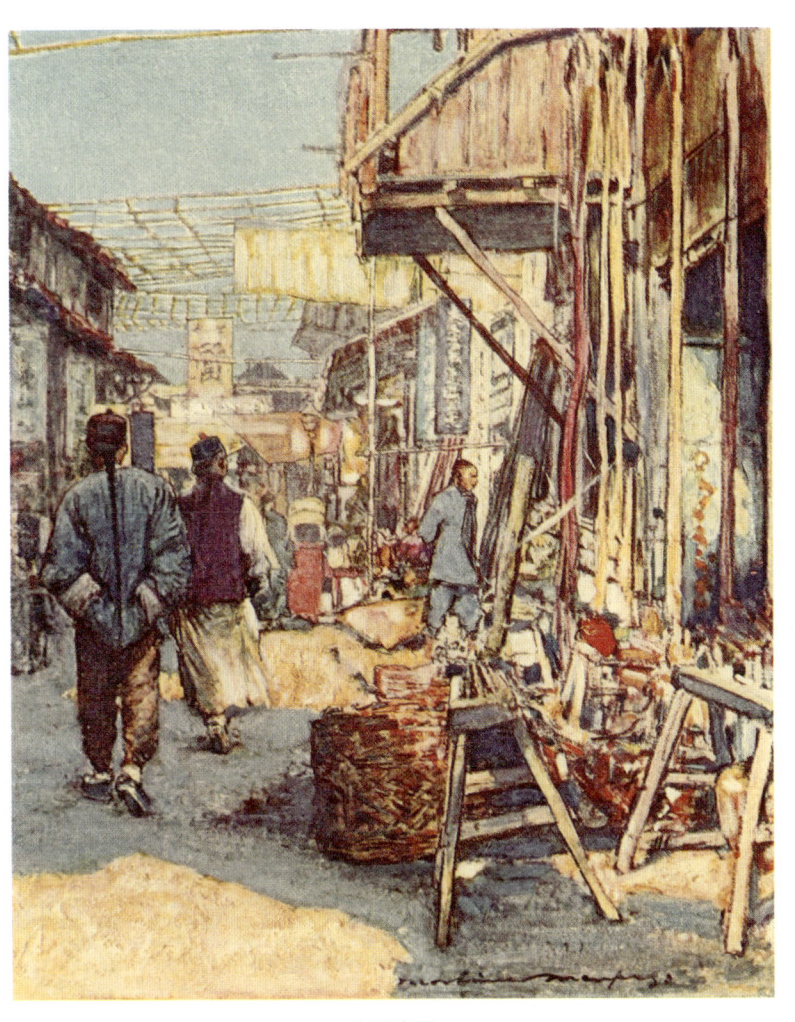

典型街景

街上的小摊

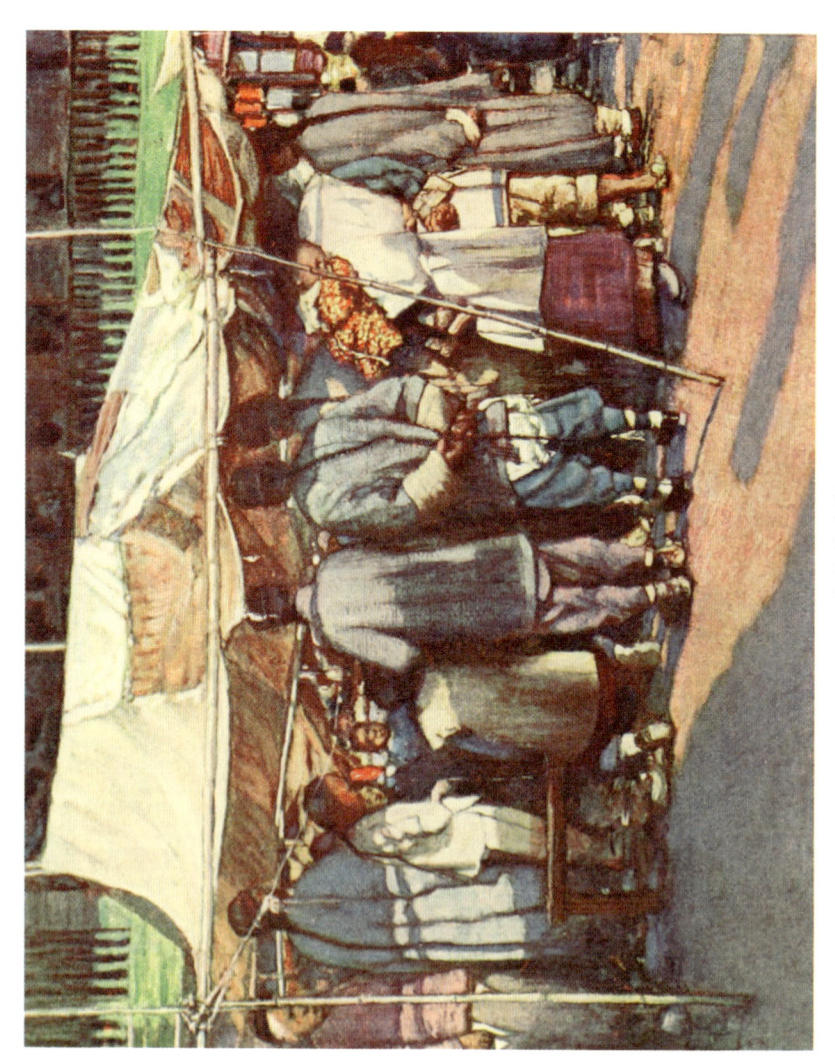

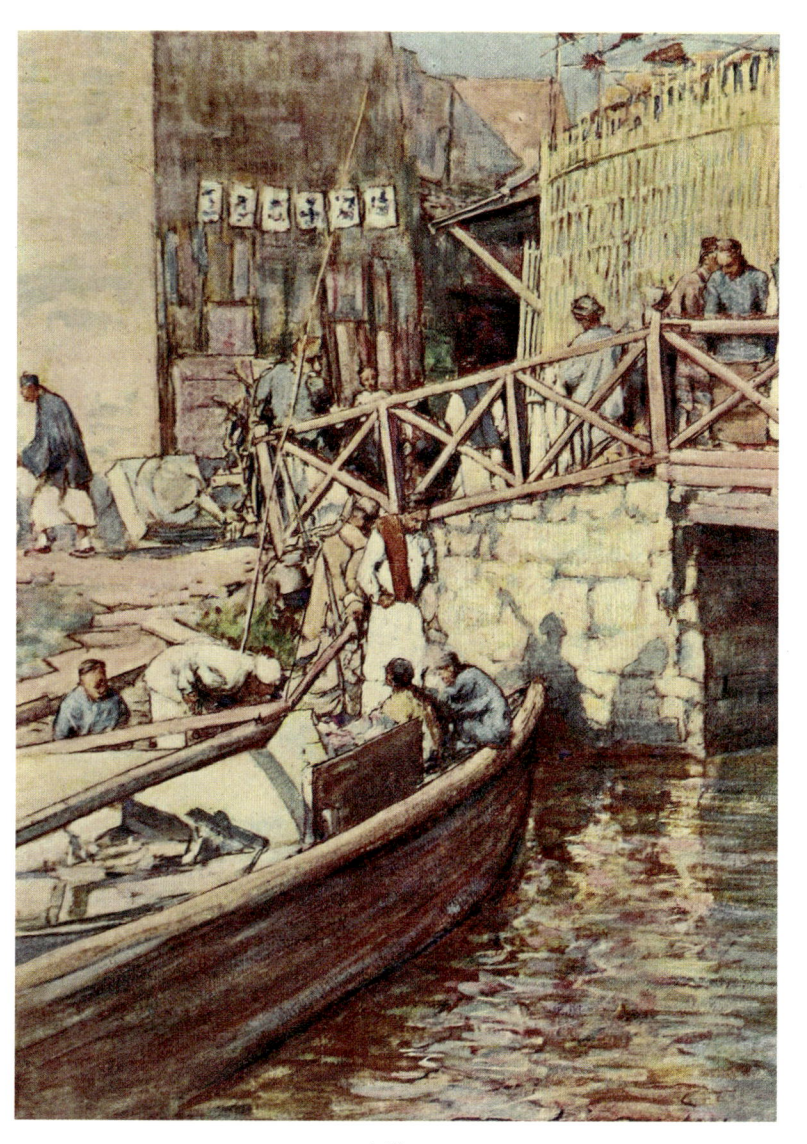

在港口

一座寺庙

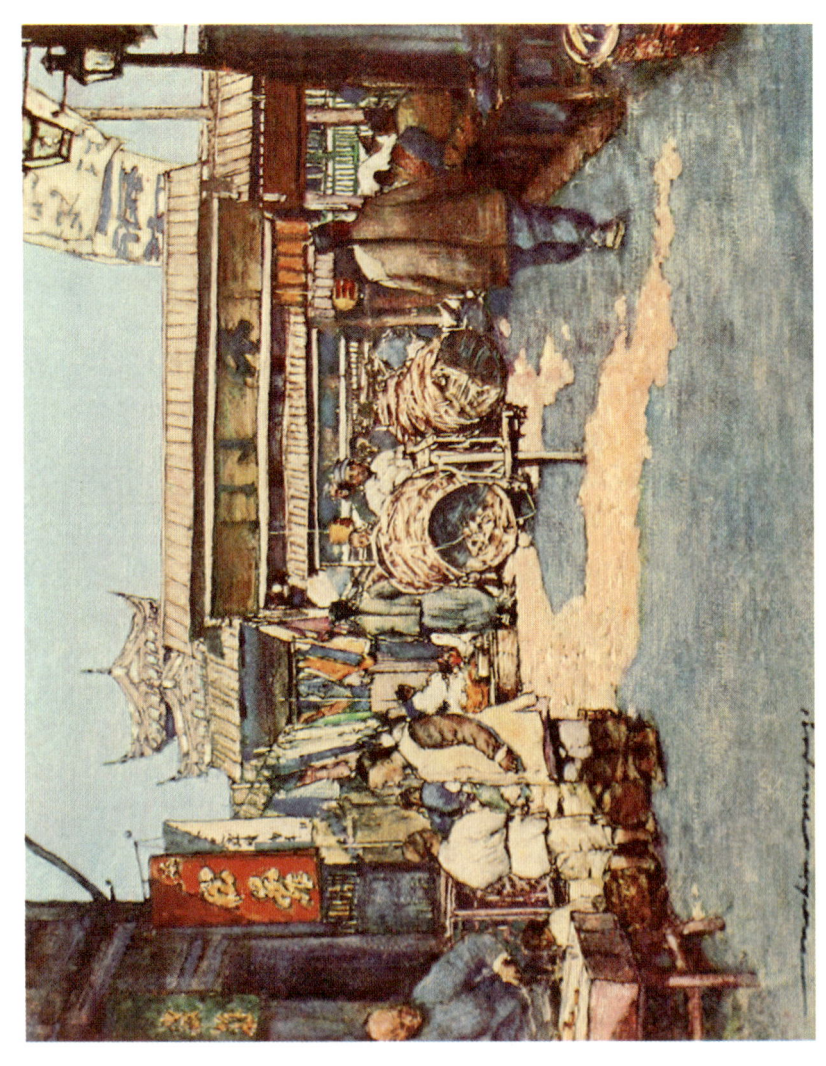

出版前言

本书作者是第十二任香港总督亨利·阿瑟·卜力。1898年6月，英国与清政府签订《展拓香港界址专条》，租借九龙以北、深圳河以南土地。5个多月后，卜力上任。卜力的到来并未受到欢迎，在收服新界的过程中与当地中国居民产生了严重冲突。此事甚至惊动了清政府，李鸿章也为此事与卜力交涉。

不过，卜力也对香港产生了某些积极影响。他曾出台措施抗击鼠疫、铺设电车轨道、在九龙兴建学校，香港人熟知的卜公花园、卜公码头也是他在任时修建。痴迷于植物学的卜力还与植物学家共同发现了一种开紫花的植物，并将它移植到香港，广泛种植，这种植物就是今日中华人民共和国香港特别行政区区旗上的紫荆花。

卜力对中国这片神秘而古老的土地有着浓厚的兴趣，在任的5年间，他走访了中国许多地区，对长江、珠江等

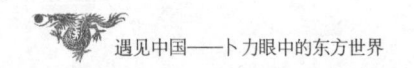

大河流域以及一些中国南方省份进行了比较周密的考察，并把所见所闻、所思所想如实地记录在本书中。他以一个西方人特有的视角对中国的传统文化、农业劳动、名胜古迹、风土人情等进行了细腻的描述，原本稀松平常的事物，经过他的描述，也增添了新的趣味。书中的彩色插图和黑白素描由英国插图画家莫蒂默·曼培斯绘制，与卜力的描述相映成趣。

卜力所处时代的中国正处于内忧外患之中，而变革的种子也开始萌发，卜力在书中也注意到了这种势头，并且也对中国的未来作出了乐观的预测，认为觉醒的中国会"加入世界商贸战场的激烈竞争……她的商业潜能巨大，生产能力也不容小觑，将来一定能自给自足，并且把自己的商品送入遥远的国外市场"。在他看来，中国的教育只要摆脱科举制度束缚，以理性的思考取代死记硬背，"中国就能够成为世界上影响举足轻重的强国"。如今，卜力的预测在一定程度上成为现实。

同时，卜力在书中也注意到当时中国存在的弊病，如裹足、卖爵鬻官等问题，为时人敲响了警钟。此外，囿于时代和身份的局限，卜力对某些事物的看法并不完全准确，如他并没有认识到中国鸦片问题的严重性，甚至认为"鸦片问题的恶劣后果通常被放大了",这反映了当时欧洲人对于此类问题的普遍看法,今日当作为史料客观看待,相信读者自然会作出正确的判断。

时过境迁,今日的中国早已与卜力笔下的中国大不相同,但100多年前的历史不会随时间的洪流而灰飞烟灭。让我们跟随卜力的文字,遇见古老的中国。

编 者

2017 年 8 月

目　录

第一章 ……………………………………………………… 1
　　中国简介—早期历史—驻军—中国军人—家庭生活—父母之权—裹足

第二章 ……………………………………………………… 14
　　婚嫁习俗—祠堂—官职等级—科举考试—税务系统—刑罚—拷问—间接证据的故事

第三章 ……………………………………………………… 30
　　中国的社会等级划分—农业—风水—当铺—河船和舢板—海宁湾浪潮—渔业—河盗—李鸿章—西江—七星山寺庙—后沥佛寺

第四章 ……………………………………………………… 51
　　长江—鸦片—新加坡委员会的结论—德国在远东地区的商贸情况—城市和农村生活—中国城市—北京—先农坛—皇帝及官员春耕仪式

第五章 ……………………………………………………… 66
　　农民—宗教信仰—戏剧—饥荒—海岸城市生活—广州—帮

派行会—丐帮—总督的公务会见—中文写作—官员生活

第六章 ·· 92

富庶之家的房屋—花艇—中国的妇女改革运动—上海妇女大会—女人的迷信—中国的女性—时尚—会友

第七章 ·· 103

香港简介—跑马地—太平山顶—海港夜景—台风—台风灾害幸存者的力量—街道—香港早晨生活掠影—中国工人—理发师—木匠—石匠—苦力—赌博—街头游戏介绍

第八章 ·· 117

龙舟赛—澳门节日—新年—新年习俗—香港赛马—奇特的赌博方式—香港慈善机构—中国的未来

第一章

要给中国作一点简单介绍，关于它的地域特征，以及我们统称为中国人的不同民族的风俗习惯，笔者因这两者的宽泛性而深感为难。中国所统治的亚洲疆域超过420万平方英里[①]，占地153万平方英里，约为英国面积的12.5倍，人口约4.1亿，为英国人口数的10倍。

---

① 平方英里，英制面积单位，1平方英里约等于259平方千米。——译者注

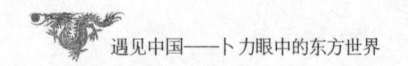

中国的西部是西藏的高山南麓区，横断山峦呈南北向，平行穿过缅甸和云南西部，萨尔温江和湄公河就是从这里发源，流向南方，黄河和长江则发源于这里的东部，灌溉着地球上最富饶的土地。

这种地势构造了一道无法逾越的屏障，人们不可能从缅甸北部城市八莫修建一条横贯中国云南高原的铁轨去四川。无论是农业还是矿产资源，四川都是所有省份中最为富庶的一个。总有一天，四川的能人们会把煤、铁、金、石油和盐都开采出来，后辈们就会发现，这些成为富翁的能人跟如今掌控西方世界命脉的资本家一样有远见卓识，才干超群。

长江以南的区域多丘陵，没有高大的山脉，长江北岸以东的区域是一片广阔而肥沃的平原，黄河就流经这里入海，长度超过500英里①，它洪水泛滥时，堪称"中国的忧患"。

在这样一个辽阔的国度里，水运是最为重要的交通方式，中国在这方面的天然优势无可匹敌。境内有3条大河，北方的黄河、中部的长江和南部的珠江。西江是

---

① 英里，英制长度单位，1英里约等于1.609千米。——译者注

珠江最大的支流。长江及其支流总长度不少于3.6万英里。居住在这三大河流域的人数有数百万之多，他们所属的民族各不相同，这也是中国人生活中最有趣的地方之一。

中国由多个不同的部族组成，其历史可以追溯至公元前2800年的伏羲时代。中国的各部族时而分裂成数个小王国，时而又因征伐的浪潮而走向统一，公元1234年，中国北方地区在成吉思汗的统治下走向统一，70年后，成吉思汗之孙忽必烈汗消灭了南宋，将中国南方的疆土也收入元朝的版图之中。正是在忽必烈统治期内，意大利人马可·波罗到访中国，从他的游记中，我们发现，那时候，远东地区（西方国家对亚洲东部地区的称呼）的经济体系就已经非常发达，中国人甚至还用上了纸币。在元大都（今北京），基督徒、阿拉伯撒拉逊人和中国占星家借用星盘来预测天气，相当于今天的气象局。

不过，在中国南方，还有些偏远地方的原住民没有与附近的其他民族居民混居。在广东和湖南两省交界的山区中，有一个彝族部落，汉族官员不得出现在他们的居住地，他们也不允许陌生人进入他们的村镇，他们的房屋都建在悬崖峭壁上，很难靠近，而且能够抵抗侵袭。他们以砍伐树木为生，冬天，他们砍下木头，涨水的时候就把木头扔到山间的溪流中，木头顺流而下。他们的风俗习惯很奇怪。但是他们不伤害女人，就算在战乱时，妇女仍然能够安全地在田地里忙碌。他们本来居住在云南和广西西部，但宋朝时被汉人赶了出去。据马端临①和其他中国史学家记载，畲族、倮倮族、苗族等（中国古代各少数民族的名字都含有轻视的意思，就像我们所称的"蛮夷"一样）少数民族，很早就居住在中国境内了，他们的历史可以追溯至6000年前，当时，来自西北部地区的华夏先祖开始在中国境内定居。原始的畲族居民逐渐被赶进了山里，他们的后裔至今都还居住在那里。他们极少与汉人通婚，汉人认为与他们通婚结合是门不当户不对的婚姻，而且还认为土著部族在面对

---

① 马端临，1254—1323年，宋元之际著名的历史学家，著作有《文献通考》等。——译者注

敌人的时候只会做懦弱的逃兵。笔者听说，彝族女性的刺绣跟汉族刺绣不同，更像是如今在巴勒斯坦的伯利恒所见的那种刺绣。他们的刺绣使用的布料都是深红色或者红黄色相间的。

忽必烈之后的数个世纪，中国又陷入了长期的混乱不和，真正验证了一句古老的中国谚语"合久必分，分久必合"，我们如今也能经常听到这句话。随后，1644年，顺治帝统一了中国，开创了清朝的统治，为了让民众臣服，清政府规定所有中国人都剃去前额的头发，后面的头发则按鞑靼人传统束成辫子——这一条规定起初遭到了强烈反抗，但后来人们都接受了，并将之作为传统习惯保留了下来。所以，到现在（笔者写作时为1909年），剃除辫子，让前额长出头发就变成了与清朝决裂的标志。1850—1867年，南方各省兴起了一场名为太平天国的运动，最终遭到英国"常胜军"将领查理·乔治·戈登和李鸿章的镇压，有2250万人因此丧生，但此后，革命者都开始将辫子剃除，让头发自由生长。

为了挽回局面，并杜绝以后民众的反叛，清朝统治者在每座大城市里都布下重防，这些防守的勇猛彪悍的将士甚至还有独立的住房，260年来，这些将士及其家人靠政府发放的米粮维持生活，他们不得进行商贸活动，也不得与汉人通婚，这样的规定造成的后果是无可避免的，他们就逐渐变成一支懒散的队伍，以往满族男性刚勇的个性已经消失，并且大部分人都不服管制，冲动好斗。直到近期，这两项禁令才得以废除，他们也会最终同化为普通民众。

从士兵接受专业训练的角度而言，这些"部队"不过是一群持有武器的暴民，对军事行动只有最基本的了解。而北方的局势危急，部队需要像西方军队一样，将各地军队集中加强训练，虽然这样的训练让军队能力增加了，但却削弱了军队的形象——因为各省都有自己的独立部队，但是人员数量不统一，质量参差不齐，人员数量多少和质量的好坏，都依据部队将领的能力和资源而定。

据称，中国军人的俸禄每月有6美元，这些钱足够他们每月的开销了，不过在实际发放的时候还会被上级正式和非正式的官员克扣大约一半。他们还能得到100

磅^①的大米,不过这些大米下发的时候,米里面还掺杂了很多沙砾和泥土。

军人的军装是一件猩红、蓝色和黑色相间的中式马褂,前后都有他的军团名号和标志物,袖子很宽,空空荡荡的;每个军团的帽子形状都不一样,有的是老式的小圆帽,有的就是一顶尖尖的盖帽,而有的军团戴的是巨大的草帽,这些帽子,除了太阳毒辣的时候,其他时间都是背在背上的;裤子都是普通的中式风格,深蓝色的,裤脚在脚踝处打了结,这种装束很适合军人,大量的军人身着这种装束的时候,场面可是相当壮观的,但不能由此得出这样的推论,说所有穿着这种衣服的人都是军队里的士兵。当军官接到上级检阅的命令时,他们总会找来很多劳动力应付。例如,要举行重大游行,部队军官就向上级提请2000人,并且要求支付2000人的日薪,而实际上部队的真实人数可能不超过300,这是一场关于财富的赌博,本质上是部队军官向上级勒索钱财,所有的中国官员都是这样做的,但他们肯定没有被发现。因此,官员们费尽心机召集了1700个苦力,全都整装待

---

① 磅,英制重量单位,1磅约等于0.45千克。——译者注

发,并且教会他们如何握枪向上级致敬,仪式结束后,这些苦力全部被遣散,武器装备和服装再次被收藏好,等待下一次召集军队的时候再用。

军官是从社会等级较高的人中选出来的,但有时候,部队抓到了特别厉害的盗贼,盗贼的勇猛受到上级赏识,这样他也能够谋得一官半职。年轻的官员都要接受一定程度的基本训练,在广州,直到近期,对军官的骑术和箭术进行年度考核才逐渐成为一种执行惯例。城郊的一个校场里,有一块约250码①的场地,被围篱围好作为训练演习的场所,围篱约5英尺②宽,2英尺深,每隔50码,就有3根软材料制作的圆柱,每根6英尺高,直径2英尺。每位应试者都骑上一匹小矮马,坐在马鞍上,他们骑马疾驰,还要努力射箭,拉满了弓,两支箭插在腰带处,沿着场中的沟渠来回跑,这沟渠显然是为了防止马由于缰绳紧勒住了脖子突然转向而挖的。应试者距离箭靶不过

① 码,英制长度单位,1码约等于0.91米。——译者注
② 英尺,英制长度单位,1英尺约等于0.305米。——译者注

两三英尺的距离,这样他们才能射中目标。3支箭都射中了箭靶的靶心,应试者才算通过了测验,坐在近旁另一个空旷场地里的长官才会向上级推荐这位应试者。然而,北方省份却不是这样的,因为这里的某些军队都经过专业训练,而且装备齐全,像欧洲军队一样。事实证明,中国军队绝不缺乏勇气,只要得到恰当的引导,如今的中国常备军能够与13世纪成吉思汗的铁骑相提并论,当时,成吉思汗的大军横扫西亚,入侵欧洲,最远打到了今匈牙利的布达佩斯。

过去,我们常说,一个帝国是由其统治者而凝聚起来的,但在中国,我们也许应该说,中国是因为普遍接受孔子的学说而凝聚起来的,孔子的著作《论语》发表于耶稣诞辰的500年前——宣扬的是人应遵循的基本品行,包括敬爱父母,敬畏君王,遵从长者和上级,以及泛爱众等理念。孔子认为,人性本善,但是"玉不琢,不成器;人不学,不知义"。

2000多年来,中国稳定的基石就在于家庭,从普通百姓之家到王公贵族之殿,全部都实行家长制。家庭由父母亲掌管,村庄由长辈管理,随后才是村长,地区由各种官吏管理,官职等级分省级官员、道台、州县官员等，象征着他们各自掌管区域的重要性，依据的管理原则都是按古老的风俗习惯而定的，而具体的管理细节还是很灵活的。在正派的中国家庭中，没有什么比孩子对父母保有虔诚的敬意更重要的了，而父母也会对孩子表示慈爱。看到一个年幼的孩子进入房间，很严肃地向父母亲磕头，这种情景真的令人震撼。如果没有父母的首肯，年轻人不敢开始吃喝，在王侯家族之中，这种礼节尤为严苛，在餐桌旁就餐时，父亲问儿子问题，回答之前儿子必须先站起来。

中国的富人通常能娶两三个甚至更多的"妻子"，我们西方人都认为这肯定会导致继承权问题，然而，事实上这却并不是什么问题，因为虽然男人可以按照风俗习惯娶多个妻子，然而法定的妻子却只有一个，而且她也是后院之首。她被称作"大夫人"，尽管她可能一生都没有孩子，不过其他"妻子"的孩子都会被视作她的孩子，而且孩子们都要对

第一章

她毕恭毕敬,而孩子自己的母亲则被称为"姨娘"。这一点在西方人看来很奇怪,然而中国上流社会的女性似乎都接受了这一点,这一风俗可能起源于人们希望儿子继承家族香火的愿望。有时候,男人可能不会娶多个妻子,但是会收养一个儿子,因此这个养子就成为家庭的长子,而且即便后来男人的妻子生了一个儿子,养长子的地位也不会因此而动摇。女儿的情况就不一样了,她不能为家庭赢得声誉,也无法为娘家传宗接代,女儿未来会成为寡妇,因此,如果家里已经诞生了一个女儿,那父亲就会作出决定,以后若再有女儿降临,那她们都不能存活下去。这个决定通常是在女婴出生之前就通过了的,因此,诞生的女婴一出生就会被按在水桶中溺死,按照中国人的观念,这孩子从没有存在过。但是,女孩一直是过着离群索居的生活,大门不出,二门不迈。这样,父亲才会像疼爱儿子一样疼爱她,在请了私家教师的家庭中,女儿们跟儿子们一起读书。

父母的权力是无限大的,甚至能决定孩子的生死。母亲杀害儿子不必担心法律惩罚,但如果孩子出于自卫杀害了父母,他就会被凌迟或千刀万剐——这种恐怖刑罚是专为背叛婚姻、杀害丈夫和父母的人而设置的。确实,从理论上而言，中国的女性被人视作"二等公民"，而发妻或正妻是整个家庭的控制者，甚至可以号令儿子的妻妾。她在家里可以独断专行，对家庭事务有相当重大的影响，甚至可以说是举足轻重。官员的妻子有权利佩戴与丈夫官位品级相当的首饰和标志物，紫禁城里的皇太后地位在帝国里是仅次于皇帝的。

不久前的一份香港报纸上，刊登了一则故事，说的是一个年轻的富人，他的母亲在广东经营大公司，而他自己花的钱也是出自母亲的公司，小车和其他奢侈品对他的吸引力很大。在用尽了各种手段控制儿子失效之后，母亲最终用上了手铐脚镣，将他锁了起来，然而，他还是逃了出去，恼怒的母亲决定，儿子一回来就砍断他脚踝的肌腱，让他变成残疾人。我举出这个故事，只是为了说明，恼怒的父母经常用这种方式对待不听话的儿子。

中国最令人无法理解的风俗就是女人要"裹足"，女性从三四岁

第一章

的时候就开始"裹足",这个过程很费事。除了大脚趾以外,其他的脚趾头都会被包裹起来,完全裹好了之后,女孩只能依靠大脚趾支撑身体行走。中国大户人家的女性外出的时候,不乘坐轿辇,就会被丫鬟背在背上或者由两名女性随员搀扶,而普通的中国女性有时也会光脚参加田间劳作。她们为什么要遭受母亲遭过的罪?她们成年后,为什么不逐渐摆脱"裹足"的束缚呢?这似乎令人很难理解。答案就在于,释放对脚的束缚也会有风险,而且奴仆也不许裹脚。这样畸形的脚就意味着女孩来自一个受人尊重的大家庭,裹脚的女孩比不裹脚的女孩更加好找婆家。这种风俗的起源已经湮没在历史的尘埃之中了。清王朝花费了巨大的努力来改变这一点,这是可以想象的,因为满族的女性并不裹脚,尽管政府出台了多项法令禁止,但这个风俗依然保留了下来。在西方人看来,中国女人的裹脚就跟欧洲人的束腹一样有害,而从生理上而言,裹脚比束腹的伤害要小得多,因为束腹不仅让人身体的骨骼变形,还会导致所有内脏都移位。

第 二 章

中国人的婚嫁习俗跟爱尔兰农民的有一点类似。男女双方婚约的磋商是由男方邀请的媒人来进行传递的,所有的礼节规矩都必须严格遵守。其中有一条无法逾越的限制性条款——新娘和新郎的姓氏不能是相同的——只有河南省除外,在河南,这一条限令无效。

我们发现,中国人口有 4 亿,然而姓氏却不超过 100 个,这也是这条限令所造成的后果。中国可能有 400 万王姓人氏,但姓王的男人不能娶这 400 万同姓氏人中的女性。婚姻是中国女性生命中的头等大事,父母会竭尽所能地操办好她的婚事。离开娘家的前一天,她的嫁妆和彩礼都会被送到婆家。几年前,广东省的一位富翁嫁女儿时，请了700名苦力来搬运这些东西，有些礼物看上去精美绝伦，非常奢华。第二天，新郎带着200人的队伍前来迎亲——有的骑着高头大马，有的配着"武器"，排成方阵形，带着喜糖，还有一群孩子，孩子的数目象征着吉祥如意。还有少不了的红灯笼，婚庆的乐队打头阵，后面跟着一条30米长的"龙"，"龙"的腿部被男孩子用木棒举起来，不断蹦蹦跳跳，给这条"龙"增添了生命的活力。

新娘乘坐的花轿经过了精美的装饰，上面还有雕花，是大红色的，翠鸟蓝色的羽毛被精心粘贴在花轿上，看上去跟瓷釉一样。抵达婆家后，新娘进门还需要进行一些仪式，要跨过门口燃烧的火盆，以求去灾辟邪。

苏格兰高地的新娘进婆家门时也会举行这样的活动，维多利亚女王的第四个女儿，被封为阿盖尔公爵夫人的路易丝公主，嫁入苏格兰王室，进入因弗拉雷城堡时也跨过火盆。

婚礼举行后的第二天，新娘就要按风俗给新郎准备早餐，生火用的木柴是她的嫁妆妆奁，因为她带到婆家的是所有生活必需品。不久前，澳门的一场婚礼后，新娘准备按风俗准备食物的时候，却惊讶地发现，娘家居

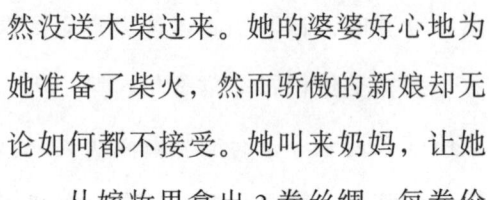

然没送木柴过来。她的婆婆好心地为她准备了柴火,然而骄傲的新娘却无论如何都不接受。她叫来奶妈,让她从嫁妆里拿出2卷丝绸,每卷价值40美元,点燃了丝绸生火做饭。后来,她的父亲过来看望她,她就把这个小插曲告诉了父亲。他说:"你做得对,我的女儿。你挽回了父亲的面子。"回家后,父亲立即派遣了100名苦力,背着木柴赶到亲家家里,而女婿家里根本放不下这么多木柴。

"闹洞房"的仪式对新娘而言有时就像一场考验,然而在富庶的家庭中,这些仪式还是很合规矩和习俗的。笔者的一位朋友婚礼后第二天晚上也进行了"闹洞房"。笔者和朋友们赶到时,女士们的饭已经吃完了,但男士们还没有吃完。这天晚上,新娘绕着被泼了烧酒的桌子行走,前一天晚上,她的婆婆已经教过她了。新娘走进"洞房",穿着大红色的喜服,嫁妆上披着大红色的长绶带,红色和金色相间的对襟开衣领,头上戴着新娘花冠。镶嵌着珍珠的喜帕从头上垂下,她面露微笑,看起来非常高兴。前一天晚上她还因为离开娘家暗自心伤,情绪低落,这时再看她的模样,我们才放下心来。男士们都回来之后,"闹洞房"也就开始了。大家给她出了很多难题,她迅速做出来的有两三个。有人出了一个复杂难解的日本谜语,但婆婆却不让新媳妇去做,因为她说那太难了。新郎进了房门,男士们提议让新郎新娘一起绕房间走一圈,然后按大家要求再绕行一圈。还有个习俗就是新娘头上的喜帕要揭开,这样大家才能一睹芳容。喜帕揭开了,然后新娘要接受婆家类似诗歌一样的考问。一位家中的男性长辈站在一旁,以评判新娘的回答是否正确。人们让新娘请求丈夫牵她的手,还要问他,娶了她之后他得到了什么,等等。新娘还要向房间里的人致敬,要向不同的人敬茶。她需要向一两个长辈磕头敬礼,还有一两个后辈要向她磕头,这当然是因为他们的辈分不同所致。对新娘的有些问题和要求太过严苛,任何年轻的女士听了都会很难受,但中国的女性却对此无所谓,这让我们这些身在中国的外国人很难理解。这种考问是为了测定新娘的脾气、个性和头脑。

在那些下层中国民众的家里,婚礼的仪式更加令人难受,因为有时候还会上演恶作剧,不幸的新娘总会受到冒

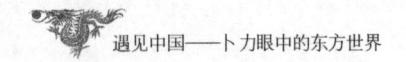

犯，被人狠命地反复捏掐。但是，面对这些粗俗难受的仪式，她不能发火抱怨，因为旁人会认为她不具备服从丈夫的品质。

每个家庭都有先祖"祠堂"，这里供奉着每一个故去家人的牌位，每天这里都会点着蜡烛，一年内，所有家庭成员都要来这里一两次，一起祭祀缅怀先祖。如果一个男人让家里蒙羞了，那么，死后祠堂里将不会供奉他的牌位，这样的后果就是，他的后辈们无法参加官方的科举测试。

家族的田地每年都会进行分配，田地的一部分收成是要用于支付当地寺庙的开销，包括那些耗巨资举办的宗教礼拜仪式，用作这部分开销的田地由家庭成员轮流看管耕种。如果佃户是基督徒，那么他就会拒绝缴纳与自己的宗教信仰相违背的寺庙的开支。而这部分费用则会分摊到其他家庭成员头上，他们就会认为基督徒给他们增添了额外的负担。这会导致家庭成员反对基督教的情绪，但中国人并不会犯宗教偏执。

中国的官阶等级划分非常严格。跟其他国家一样，中国也是专制统治的国家，在特定的范畴之内，每个官员自己就是一部法律。因此，每一个有野心的男孩都梦想当官。

各省会每3年在省首府举行一次会试,有15万—20万考生参加,这些考生都是省内各地每年参加乡试成功夺得优胜名次的人。为了参与科举考试,考生必须携带身份证明,以证明自己来自当地声誉在外的家庭,如果没有成功通过,那他以后还得参加每3年一次的会试,从这里,我们也能明白家族祠堂里牌位的重要性。强盗、戏子和船夫是不能参加科举的。

在广州、南京和其他大城市里,还能看到这些考试贡院和号舍——进入这些场所之前,考生都要经过严格搜身,以确保他们没有携带任何纸片或其他写有文字的东西用以作弊。广东省内的考试场所超过1.1万处,而南京的则更多。这些小单间都是并排而建的,宽度3.8英尺,长度5.9英尺,前方墙壁高6英尺,后方高9英尺。在这个房间里,除非是通知考官不再继续考试,否则考生不得随意走动,而且很多人在考试时死去。在南京,每次科举考试平均每天有25个考生死亡。

那些在考场中拔得头筹的人会马上被封官,并且在家乡赢得名声。而那些没能拔得头筹而成绩也还算优秀的人则被分派到不同的省份,由政府出资侍奉,以待官位空缺。一旦得到了任命,他们就可能被提拔到道台的地位上,县州级长官乃至总督等。在这些官级提拔中，钱起了重要的作用，一个富翁可以不经考试买个一官半职，在文化更先进的国度里，这种事也是稀松平常的。在某些情况下，如果一个男孩在学业上显现出极高的天赋和智慧，那他的家庭就会竭尽财力支持他念书。如果他功成名就，获得了重要的官职，他的家庭也就得到了回报，跟他一起分享荣华富贵，家族的名声也得到了宣扬。这整个接受教育、参加考试的过程就是填鸭式的教育，英国人也从中国人这里学到了这种竞争考试的方式。

通过考试获得我们俗称的"秀才"，尽管他没有获得官职，但他从此不再从事体力劳动，无论他出身多么贫困潦倒，此后他就属于学术界的绅士了，居住地发生的大小事务，他都可以干预。要了解他们如何生活并不容易，而中国人，就跟其他东方国家的人一样，都非常尊重文化人，并且也没有开化到为了财富而放弃更高追求的地步。这种人可能适合负责他们当地的社会经济工作，当然，这些人之中也有些懒虫，他们想得到正常的工作，却迷上了吸食鸦片，这样的人就是民众中的"蛀虫"。

省里的总督其实是半独立性质的官职。一个6000万人的省份，名义上，总督每年年度经费可获得1000—2000英镑，他必须要用这些俸禄养军队，沿海省份的还包括海军，还要用于税务和行政开支。

税率都是由总督决定，只有农民的谷种缴纳的税除外，这就相当于地税。付了地税之后，小农的生活就完全不受官方压迫了，在中国，这种人只要勤劳忠诚，就比其他的农民要更加自由。

这种征地税的方式很独特，从远古时代就存在了。地税的征集不是按土地面积来算的，而是按产量来计算的，两块同样面积的土地，一块土壤肥沃的可能可以产出两蒲式耳①的谷物，而另一块土壤贫瘠的土地上，栽种间隙更宽，所以可能只能产出1蒲式耳的谷物。所有种子都由官方采购，他们会根据各户的用量，计算出应缴的税。同样的原理也适用于距离的量算，假设上山和下山用的力气和时间比率相同，那么上山的距离若算作10里②，那么下山

---

① 蒲式耳，容积单位，1英制蒲式耳约等于36.37升。——译者注
② 里，国内长度计量单位，1里等于0.5公里。——译者注

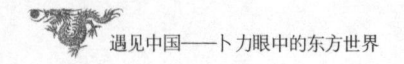

的距离则只有5—6里。

除了种子税，还有一种厘金，或称货物过境税，是针对各地货物运输而征收的税，商人还要缴纳商品的各种课税。商人通过经商积累了一定的财富，挥霍无度的话，很快钱就会被用光，如果他去贷款，想东山再起，肯定会遭到拒绝，贷款给他的人要冒着很大的风险，因为他再没有能力偿还自己的债务，贷款方会考虑贷款额是否超过了限度，贷款人是否有偿还能力。所有人都知道，缰绳拉到什么程度会崩断。如果商务税务负担过重，人们就会拉好窗帘，拒绝做生意。如果这样的状况持续了一段时间，那么总督就会被撤职。几年前，广州总督想要征收新税，因此就出现了人们拒绝从商的现象，人们一直坚持，最终总督便放弃了征税。

所有的官员都在一定的范围内接受了总督的行事原则，民众似乎也能够理解并接受，从整体上而言，在日常生活中，执法情况还是令人满意的。

当然，凡事都有例外。在广东省，一位居住在乡间的富翁家里遭到了一群持有武器的强盗的洗劫。富翁坚决保卫自己的家，强盗撤离的时候，富翁杀了3个强盗。然而，事情到这里还没完，因为愤愤不平的盗贼上书给地方官控告富翁，并且贿赂了地方官，地方官于是传唤被盗的富翁进衙门，富翁应命过来了，害怕得瑟瑟发抖。他还没见到地方官，就被迫缴纳了150美元，而地方官也并没有赞赏他的勇敢，反而是不断责备他，并且还命令富翁为3个死去的盗贼承担丧葬费用。支付给每个人的费用由法院裁决，这种赔付制度，地方官及其下级似乎都违反了公正原则，但是，某位接受过高等教育、拥有苏格兰大学学位的中国官员，他曾经在香港受殖民统治时期任职，在谈到这个话题时声称，他宁愿在中国而不愿在英国的法院审理案件，因为，在中国的法院里，他明白自己要付出的是什么，而在受殖民统治的法庭中，如果他想用钱摆平案件，律师们就不会放过他。

九龙地区被划入受殖民统治地区（之前当地居民进行过武装反抗，因为他们认为改易旗帜会让他们遭遇不幸）时，当地成立了法院，简易裁判权交给了当地首领，法院里还坐着英国的官员，不过还有一条限制性条款，律师和法务官不得进入这些法院，这是经过双方集会争论，然后由英国官员裁定执行的。

中国法院的惩罚是非常严苛的，有时候会让人心生恐惧。小罪过的惩罚通常是枷刑和笞刑。枷是一种3英寸长的木板，面积3平方英尺，中间有一个圆孔，用以套住囚犯的头。枷被套到囚犯头上时，囚犯就会被带到法庭门外，他犯的罪过都写在枷板上，有的时候，他还要全城游行。这种情况下，他自己不能进食，因为他的手无法碰到头，也没有办法好好躺下休息，有时候，双手也被束缚在枷上。这种刑罚比我们教会的足枷更加严厉，但理念是相同的。就像一只讨厌的骚扰中国人的蚊子，它的力量有多大呢，其实一点也不大，但如果这只蚊子总是来骚扰，也会让人非常难受。

答刑跟枷刑又不一样，就是用一根粗大的竹竿或两根细小的竹条施加刑罚。答刑是让囚犯脸朝下趴着，一人按住双脚，另一人按住头。粗大的竹竿看起来很可怕，不过虽然人用力击打，但不会伤到骨头，只会留下轻微的皮外伤。细小的竹条用法就不一样了，行刑者双手各握一支竹条，坐下来疯狂抽打罪犯，几乎不停歇。前五六十次，犯人并没有什么严重的不适，而且身体的皮肤也没有受伤，然而经过不

第二章

断抽打，皮肤下的组织被破坏了，犯人感觉非常疼。经过这种严刑峻罚，衣物也被破坏掉了，而且伤口的恢复也很缓慢。

然而，这些处罚还算轻量级的，现在，为了得到关键的证据，犯人还得承受更严重的折磨，按照沿袭到现代的风俗，除非罪犯亲口承认犯下了深重的罪行，否则不得执行死刑。有时，犯人受刑严重，对自己的案件已经非常失望，想要速死摆脱痛苦而承认罪行，否则是很难"法外开恩"的。必须承认的是，通过折磨犯人，得到了宝贵的证据，可能已经能够完全证明犯人的罪行，但通常这样的证据是完全不可信的。

一位跟某些重要人士有私交的中国绅士曾告诉过我以下的故事。

来自两个富有家族的一男一女结婚了。婚礼过后的当晚，新娘和新郎回到自己的房间休息，这个房间是主屋外的一个独立房间。躺下休息后不久，他们就听到头顶传来了声响，新郎起了床，穿好红色喜服，点起一支蜡烛，爬上阁楼去查看情况。在阁楼上，他发现了一个盗贼，是通过屋顶的洞进来的，盗贼察觉到自己被发现了，于是跟新郎展开了一番打斗，过程中，盗贼将一把刀捅进了新郎体内，杀了他。然后盗贼穿上新郎的服装，手里拿着蜡烛，胆大包天地回到房间里，此时，新娘还在等着丈夫回来。由于婚前新郎新娘没有见过面，而且新娘此时焦虑不安，因此她并没有发现，下来的这位并不是她的新婚丈夫。他告诉她，他发现一个盗贼潜入房间里，而盗贼一发现他就逃了出去，还说家里出现了盗贼，新娘最好将身上的珠宝交给他，他会把珠宝存放到父亲的房间里去，以确保安全。新娘听话地交出了价值数千两银子的珠宝，然后盗贼走了出去，带着珠宝离开了。

第二天一早，新郎的父亲过来看望儿子，但新娘却告诉他，新郎说要确保财产安全，就带着她的珠宝离开了，而且一直没回来。新郎的父亲听了前一天晚上发生的事，赶到阁楼去查看，结果却发现了儿子的尸体。他找遍了家里所有地方，只在某个院子外发现了一只陌生的鞋子。

这个家族的一些朋友参加了婚礼之后就留在了这家里。其中有一个年轻人，是一个饱读诗书的学者，而且很受人尊重。新郎的父亲拿着陌生的鞋子跟所有刚刚起床的宾客的鞋子比对。比对时,他发现,那位饱读诗书的年轻人一只脚上穿着跟手中的鞋子一模一样的鞋子,另一只脚上则穿着被害死了的儿子的鞋子。这位父亲是个很谨慎的人,因此他并没有马上下令捉人,而是转向了刚过门就守了寡的儿媳,并问了她一些问题。他问她是否能辨认出那个假扮成她新婚丈夫的人,她回答不能,他要求她仔细回想一下,随后进门的那个男人有没有什么明显的特征以确认身份,仔细回忆了一会儿,她回答说"有",她记起来,那个人缺了一个拇指。父亲回到了宾客所住的房间,问那位年轻人为什么穿着儿子的鞋,年轻人说,晚上,他出门溜达,在经过某个院子的时候失足摔了一跤,在黑暗中丢了一只鞋,于是随手捡拾了一只套上,还以为是自己的鞋。新郎的父亲检查他的双手,发现果然少了一根拇指,于是他不再怀疑,马上报官,并将年轻人扭送到官府里。年轻人坚决不承认自己谋杀了新郎,声称自己也是有妻有儿的人,而且家境不错,也是被害的新郎的好朋友。但他还是被关进了牢房,受了一番折磨之后,他坦白确实杀害了新郎。新郎遗体已经仔细核验过了,伤口的深度也进行了测量和记录。被问及他是怎样处理那把杀害了新郎的刀,还有那些珠宝的去向时,他却回答不能说,尽管已被酷刑折磨得只剩一口气,最后还被砍了头。但是,他的叔叔和妻子不相信他犯了罪,他们向所有权贵送礼求情,要求还年轻人清白,他们声称,除非找到了那把刀和那些珠宝,否则不能判刑,但是官员却不听他们的。最终,他们告到了总督那里,总督听说了他们的事,于是说,他们坚决请愿洗刷罪名,是很勇敢的行为。总督传唤了被害人的父亲和妻子,他们复述了事情的来龙去脉,那已经变成了证实那个年轻人罪名的最可靠证据。总督问那位妻子,她是否还记得那名盗贼是哪只手上缺了大拇指,她回答说:"当然,我记得很清楚,是右手。"然后他传唤了那名嫌疑人的妻子,问她丈夫是哪只手没有大拇指。她回答说:"左手。"随后总督又传唤了新郎的父亲,问他是否认识别的缺了拇指的人。他回答说,两年前,他的一个仆人因行为不检点而被他解雇了,那名仆人也缺了一个大拇指。总督又问,婚礼期间有没有见过那位仆人,新郎的父亲回答说见过,不过自那之后就再也没见过了。

第二章

　　然后总督又对那名仆人进行了调查，那名仆人已经移居到了另一个省份，而且生活富足，还开了一家颇具规模的店铺。随后，那名仆人被逮捕了，在严刑的折磨下，他承认了罪行，并且还说出了藏匿刀子的地点和珠宝的去向。那把刀的刀刃很宽，与尸体上的伤痕吻合，一部分珠宝被追了回来，其他有的被当掉了，有的被卖掉了。地方官被降了职，并且因为没有找到刀和珠宝这两件关键证据而处死无辜的人而缴纳罚金。

　　这个案子表明，间接证物找不到是很不利的，从实用主义的角度证实了刑讯制度的成功和失败之处。我在香港主政时期，一直令我深感满意的是两名杀人凶手自首的案件，经过公正的审问证实有罪，由于有可靠的证据佐证，我让当时的总督打破古老的惯例，无须让犯人关押受罚，直接处死，尽管他们到最后关头都不认罪。一旦开了先例，野蛮的刑讯制度将不再使用，我希望，在罪犯处理这方面，中国能够像世界上的其他文明国家一样，摆脱残暴的不公平，也免除人们遭受的苦难。

第 三 章

中国的社会阶级划分如下：

第一级：士（文人），因为思想比物质更为重要。

第二级：农（农民），因为他在田地里耕种，获得粮食。

第三级：工（工匠），因为他用原材料制作出生活用品。

第四级：商（商人），因为人们能从他这里获得生活生产所需要的物品。

第五级：兵（士兵），因为他就是个破坏者。

这种划分从表面上看符合逻辑，但是，我们从中可以看出，中国人根本没有意识到军队是国家安全的保障，反而认为军队会摧毁其他几个阶级的生存，而这种谬论已经渗入人们的思想之中。因为最近数年，中国出现了各种"军队"，而这些所谓的"军队"不过是一群没有原则纪律的武夫，他们的军官，正如我之前所说的那样，有时候是因勇猛过人而获得宽恕的强盗，而且获得了管理所谓的士兵的指挥权。而现在，这种局面得到了改观，袁世凯和张之洞（湖广总督）的军队就是训练有素、管理到位的。在中国，士人一直都蔑视军人，总督张之洞就采用了一种行之有效的方法，用以对抗士人对军人的蔑视。他还创建了海军和农业学堂，以及教授地理、历史、数学的学堂，并且将学生编入后备军队。我在汉口的时候，张之洞总督还邀请我去参观他创建的8000人的军队，这支部队当时正在汉口附近地区演习，我到达他们驻地的时候，这支后备部队的百人仪仗队出来迎接我，他们一身戎装，有礼有节，我对他们印象深刻。他们的穿着十分精致，武器装备也很不赖，确实是正规军队的模样。总督指派麾下的一名德裔将领带我参观他们的演习,我一点也不怀疑,那些现在就成为实习军官的学生们,将来一定能提高整个军队的素质。

每年,在北京的先农坛,皇帝都会在所有王公贵族和高级官员的陪同下,犁出三道沟,随后,王公贵族也开始犁地。整个中国约有 9/10 的人口都以农业为生,世上没有哪个国家比中国的土壤肥力保持得更好。我走过中国这么多地方,没有见到过荒地,乡间各处的田地里都栽满了谷物蔬菜,盛产丝绸的地方种着桑树,还有大量的粉色和白色的荷花,它的籽和块茎状的根都可以食用,宽大的叶子可以做包装。城镇乡村都不兴浪费,所有可以做肥料的东西都可以回归到土壤里。在中国,没有被城市下水道污染的河流,运河的河岸上,农民甚至会用各种独特的工具疏浚河流,把水引进自家的田地里。

农民居住在村庄里,每个村都有自己的村长和元老,所有村民都对他们非常恭顺。有时候,两个村庄会因为地界或其他小问题产生纷争,在这种情况下,如果元老无法平息纠纷,那么纷争就可能导致战争,引发多人死亡。没有人干预,纠纷就会变成武装冲突。

因此,缺少当地政府部门干预就存在着缺陷。糖会吸引蚂蚁,财物放在家里,就会吸引盗贼,没有政府部门管辖,强抢强盗发生的频率很高。通常强盗都携带武器,他们可不介意在谋财的同时害命。这些攻击并不仅限于偏远的农村地区。广州的某位丝绸商人非常有钱,在乡间建了一栋防御性很强的别墅,数月前,这栋别墅遇到了一次袭击,商人特地加强了防御措施,给家臣们准备了大量枪炮。25艘船上载了300多个强盗沿着河流而上,他们想洗劫商人的别墅。冲突于下午6点开始,持续了7个小时,最后,别墅坚实的大门被大炮炸开,强盗们占据了房屋,带走了价值8万美元的财物,房主和他的两个儿子被掠走了,强盗们将他们当作人质,向他们的家人索要赎金。冲突中,房主的几位家人和13名强盗被杀。

乡村的居民都很迷信,非常不喜欢可以俯瞰整个村庄的建筑物,因为他们说,这样的建筑不合风水,也即自然之力。这种迷信观念给铁路和其他工程建设带来了麻烦,

这些观念由风水师传播开来,他们神秘的工作包括为家庭坟地选择合适的地方,重要人士的尸体可能存放多年不下葬,直到风水师找到合适的墓地位置,而这些位置通常在山坡上。他们还会为婚礼的举办挑选良辰吉日。香港和广州通电报的时候,某地的村民纷纷强烈反对在村里的某地树电报杆,因为他们说,这会扰乱村里的风水。幸好负责的工程师知道这些中国人的迷信信仰,他没有反驳,而是掏出双筒望远镜,仔细看了看地面,然后说:"你们说得对,我很高兴风水师为我指出了这一点,这里不是个好地方。"然后他再次用上了望远镜,查看了其他几个他原本没有打算树电报杆的地方。最后,他去了距原来的地点20码远的一个地方,发现那里跟之前那个地方一样适合施工,仔细勘察了一番之后,他长叹一口气:"啊,这个地方也很棒,我很高兴。"终于,再没有人反对,而电报杆也被安置好了。

尽管经常有强盗,但却没有什么毛贼,在小城镇里,人们会依靠当地的"警官",他被雇用时要作出保证:如果有偷盗发生，他要为损害作出赔偿。在小偷小盗的案子上，这样是很有效的。

为了确保村庄不受外来的袭击，乡村大都用高墙围住，这样就能避免小型袭击侵扰。在某些村庄里，墙上还架着古老的枪。

城镇的繁荣程度可以通过当铺显示出来，当铺通常都有坚固的高塔，防御性很强。中国的当铺跟西方国家的很不一样，因为它不仅是人们以物换钱的地方，也是闲置物品的储存所。夏天时，中国人不将冬天的衣物放在家里，冬天时也不将夏天的衣物放在家里。季节更换了，衣服也换掉了，换下的衣物就会被当掉，这样的处理方式是为了确保价格昂贵的衣物安全。如果手里没有多余的钱，在季节转换前，将合适的衣物当掉，去赎回已经典当掉的衣服。有时候，当铺老板会留下一些价值昂贵的珠宝和瓷器，他的店铺里不时会出现一些有趣的东西。

地位仅次于农业的就是渔业，中国的渔业人口有数百万之多，其中大部分是河船人口，他们的家就在船上。中国的船有多种类型，港口和大江大河上通行的数万只船的舷板承载量从5—500吨不等，大江和运河岸上的城镇还有船屋、花船、船上餐厅和音乐厅、客船、渔船、商船，等等。在这些船上,家庭从摇篮到坟墓都生活在船上,母亲忙碌的时候,小孩子可能在船上爬来爬去,用一根粗绳束缚住他,背上还绑着一个葫芦,万一掉到水里了,这个葫芦还会漂浮在水面上,以等待人发现将绳子拉回来。据统计,香港港口约有3万渔民,母亲摇桨时,将小婴孩背在背上,小孩子的头完全暴露在烈日下,在母亲背上摇来摇去,让人怀疑小孩的头会不会飞出去。

大船的船尾很高大,舷板呈流线型,夕阳的余晖照在黄色的竹席编成的风帆上,这样的画面会引出艺术家的灵感。海上或河上的江洋大盗跟岸上的劫匪一样危险,西江上的大盗就是臭名昭著的。船上晚上是不点灯的,以防止遭到盗贼袭击,但这样会增加撞船的风险,日落后在中国南方的海域里行船,船家要提高警惕才行。这些船只装载着沿河以及海岸周边城镇里出来的所有货物，抵达贸易港口，中国和外国的所有商贸活动都在贸易港口举行。方形的大船尾为船员提供了食宿之所，但没有人胆敢坐在船首。

春分时节，我们通过运河去杭州，途中，我们停在了海宁，看到滔天大浪从海湾涌向河流，这真是世界上最壮观的景象。我们得到了船主许可，正准备在船首做个标记以测量海浪的高度，一位男士坐到船首，船主很恼怒地拽着他离开，并要求他下船。我们的翻译这时赶了过来，听恼怒的船主说明了事情的经过，船主声称，船首的位置至关重要，他要在这里烧高香保佑船只顺利通行，人坐在这里一定会带来厄运，甚至可能造成船毁人亡的悲剧。随后，那位男士对自己居然无视这一点进行了辩解和道歉，最后还花了一点钱来表示和解。我们上船，要向船尾甲板触帽，也是出于同样的道理，以前，船舷板上还会置放十字架。

上文所提及的海湾里的浪头距河岸约6英里，水墙汹涌而至，10分钟之前我们就听到了它的咆哮声，前方的浪头约10英尺高，水流速度每小时14英里，然而浪头后的大海上有比尼亚加拉大瀑布更加壮观的景象。我准确测量了水流的速度和浪头的高度，1分钟内，从海宁往北100英里的海堤上浪头就升到了 9 英尺 9 英寸，海堤高度 17 英尺，用裸石堆砌而成，海堤顶端还有沉重的石头（4 英尺长，1 英尺宽），用铁制的夹钳契合到一起，跟我后来在毗邻山海关海域的长城末端的石头差不多。

如果说中国的土地上没有未经开垦的荒原，那么也可以说水都不是未经探索的死水，因为海里、河里、湖里甚至是池塘里，只要有水淌过的地方，人们就会动用想象力，制造任何可能的器具捕鱼，捕获的大部分鱼都被送上餐桌。没有比渔业规模更大的了，一口小鱼塘甚至比大它 10 倍的耕种地更有价值。有时候，鱼塘属于某个村庄，从鱼塘边的水草到丝绸产区的蚕粪便，无不是用来养鱼的，而村庄的公用厕所通常都建在鱼塘边，这也就不难理解，为什么来华的欧洲人总是不吃池鱼，而更喜欢新鲜的海鱼。这些池塘里的鱼长势很快，渔民用各种各样的渔网捕捉它们。有时候，一张 40 平方英尺的网，用竹篾片、绳索和滑轮固定，将网放到水里，过了一段时间，鱼就会游到网内，慢慢抬起网，鱼留在网里，边沿不断有水滴下。大鱼塘里，可能见到四五十人一起捕鱼，用的渔网从 12 到 15 平方英尺不等。整个池塘都被设下渔网，鱼儿不停游动，大量的鱼都落入渔网中。如果池塘靠近河边，河边又停满了船，那这些活蹦乱跳的鱼儿很快就会被运到集市上去。夏天的时候，海湾沿岸布满了不计其数的大渔网，偶尔能看到 80 平方英尺的正方形渔网，网的四角被固定在两根长竹竿的顶端，竹竿长度要与水深成比例，其他边缘都用重物固定住。捕鱼的人们待在很重的长木棒搭建的小屋里，用绑在东南西北四个角上的绳索来确保安全。在木筏上，渔网被挂在用绞盘吊起的绳索上。渔网被拉上来时，鱼就掉到了网中间的一个小袋子里，此时，并排站在悬在半空的网下的人们移开了网，让鱼从袋子里掉到船上。这些网有时也会深入水下 9—10 英寻[①]。除了在中国，我没在

[①] 英寻，海洋测量中的长度单位，1 英寻 =6 英尺 =1.8288 米，标准称号为寻。——译者注

其他国家见到过这样使用的渔网。在我们国家的海水中，我们能看到很多的海草，能闻到海水的气息，品尝到海盐的滋味，而在中国，这些都做不到。

中国人捕鱼的方式多种多样，从上述的大渔网到沟渠和存水湾里设置的小陷阱等，而且还不止如此，长江流域的宜昌城里，还有人训练水獭将鱼赶到渔网里；在湖上或运河上，航行的船上通常有8只鸬鹚，只要渔人一声令下，它们就会潜入水里去捕鱼。有时候，鸬鹚不听话，人只要用长竹竿在鸬鹚附近的水面拍打几次，鸬鹚就会立刻钻入水中捕鱼。捕到鱼之后，鸬鹚回到船上，渔民在鸬鹚面前放一只篮子，将它的下颌掰开，鱼儿毫发无损地从鸬鹚嘴里滑落，鸬鹚之所以没有吃掉捕到的鱼，是因为它的脖子下方绑了一圈绳子。

但最有趣的捕鱼方式在珠江及其支流西江上，贫穷的渔民坐在又长又窄的小船船尾，旁边挂着一块被涂成了白色的木板，晚上，渔民将木板调整到合适的角度，想要跳起来咬它的鱼就会刚好落到船里。在挪威峡湾，渔夫捕鱼的方式也差不多,将小艇停在岩石峭壁旁,在岩石峭壁上挂个篮子或者迎风系张渔网,用白色的石灰浆将篮子或网边的石块涂白,鱼儿误以为这些白色的痕迹是瀑布,于是就朝白色痕迹那里跳,结果就掉落在下面的渔网或篮子里。

内陆水域的船民也可能跟陆地上的居民一样有被持械抢劫的风险,河盗也给渔民造成了很大的困扰。就连在欧洲船员的操控下,往来于西江河面上的美式大船也不总是安全可靠的,但大家来来往往都非常谨慎。如果河盗知道船上有贵重物品,他们有时会假扮成乘客上船,按事前约定时间,掏出枪来,挟持船长和船员,另一部分河盗驾船跟随,假扮成乘客的河盗得手后,带着获得的赃物逃到同伙的贼船上。因此,客船后都不拖驳船,以防那些盗贼上船。所有中国人使用的大型蒸汽船上,下层甲板跟其他高层甲板是用铁栅栏和紧锁的大门分隔开来的,或者有一名手持武器的保安站在下层甲板上,这都是为了防盗。6年前的一天傍晚,两艘客船约定一起从香港赶往西江,进入珠江河口的内伶仃岛北部。出于某些未知的原因,第一艘船改道往内伶仃岛的南部地区航行,于是,第二艘船的船长认为,第一艘船肯定遭遇了盗贼劫掠，所以他也改变了航道，拉响了汽笛，并朝第一艘船开火。看到这种情况，第一艘船也认为第二艘船遭遇了劫掠，并准备袭击自己。第一艘船的船长又改道返回香港，一边航行一边开枪回击，双方的枪战一直持续，直到两艘船返回香港的港口，他们遇到了警用船，这时他们才发现自己弄错了。双方开了300多枪，幸运的是并没有人被击中。不到一年前，一支由七八艘船屋组成的船队，由一艘在杭州和苏州之间的运河航行的汽船引领，船上都载满了乘客，但是后来被河盗劫持了，他们洗劫了船队，就像美国西部各州的火车上不时会遭到盗贼袭击。这些不法之徒的所作所为，都是因为政府忽视了为保障公民生命财产安全而配置警力的首要职责，在恰当的管理下，大部分中国人生来是安分守己、温良恭顺的。除了主要城市外，中国的其他地方体系通常没有考虑到警务安保措施。小村庄里会自行安排治安人员，如果发生了更加严重的冲突，却缺乏特定的军队来通过官方途径处理。政府没有行之有效的管理原则，只是加大了处罚力度，犯罪之后的惩罚对那些坏蛋而言只是威慑手段。因此，省总督如果能力强，他管辖的省份就会风平浪静。有人向李鸿章提出管理一个以匪巢著称的城镇的建议,他却很平静地回应道:"我们会消灭他们的。"李鸿章是两广总督,在两广地区统治很严格,却让广州城里的富人随时都要担心财产和生命安危,使他深感遗憾。

李鸿章是中国最有能力的官员之一,他获得了俄国人的青睐。如果"义和团"运动在酝酿时,他不在广州,而是在天津或北京,那这场密谋起义可能不会达到难以控制的程度。当时,"大刀会"运动已经在江苏和湖北两省拉开了帷幕,但驻守南京和汉口的两江总督和湖广总督仍维持着省内的安定,而李鸿章甚至比他们两位还要更强势。李鸿章离开广州,准备去北京处理"义和团"事件,然而为时已晚,中国政府已经联合了外国势力一起处理"义和团"的问题。如果留在他曾严厉而有效治理的那些动乱的南方省份,他会做得更好。"义和团"运动影响非常广泛,它显示出中国各地希望团结抗外的决心。运动在北方爆发的时候,天津大学有大量的广州学生,他们就像在中国的外国人一样,生命安全得不到保障。广州某些富人因为无法带儿子离开天津,非常担心,希望我能出面帮忙。他们请求我尽力争取让英国领事带他们的儿子离开,只要领事租船让学生离开天津,就承诺送价值1万美元的任何东西给我们。我发电报给英国领事,确定了人数和钱数,他很仁慈地提供了一艘船,特许运送这些年轻人,那些向我求助的中国富人立刻送上了一张超过9000美元的支票。

在中国,各省使用的方言都不一样,过去的许多个世纪,因为语言的不通,打斗和冲突不断。直到今日,汕头的船在香港港口靠岸卸货,港口要雇用很多汕头的苦力,如果港口的苦力都是广州人,那港口就可能因为语言不通陷入混乱中,在货物卸载完成之前可能还会发生打斗。

在中国旅行的人一定会对其广袤的疆土印象深刻,这片土地上,土壤肥沃,江河纵横交错,桥梁坚固精美,城墙厚重敦实,城市中富丽堂皇与肮脏污秽形成鲜明对比,人们不知疲倦地劳作。更令人赞赏的是他们炉火纯青的手工艺。

沿着西江往上游行进,穿过一座座峡谷,我们能看到丰富多彩的中国水中世界。在引起外国人注意的江河中,西江仅次于长江,因为这里也是河盗最经常出没的地方。实际上,数年之前,如果不支付被勒索的金额并插上暗示已付钱款的旗子,中国的船不可能安然通过河流。也许河上最有趣的船要算明轮船了,是由人力驱动的,16位船夫像踏车一样踩踏着明轮,还有4位轮换者等在一边。这种工作很辛苦,做这种苦力活的劳动力寿命不长,而在中国,无论是船主还是劳工们都不会考虑这一点。在宽阔的江河里,经常能看到木筏在浑黄的水中缓缓前行——木筏约三四百码长,驾木筏的人们舒服地住在上面;大帆船上则有像纸扇一样形状如画的风帆;在每一个小镇上,都有大量的"小船",即舢板船,这种船的船头有一个活动顶棚,乘客们就坐在这里边。中国海关的主要关口就设在三水城的河道上,一只载着12人的龙舟驶出来了,船上有一把大红伞和一面绿色的旗帜,这把伞是荣誉的象征,旁边则画着象征船主的尊贵标记。在这里,40码1卷的泰清竹席售价10美元。

峡谷是从广利岛附近开始的,西江就是通过这道峡谷流向平原区而注入大海的。广利岛上有150多座小山丘,峡谷和陡峭的山谷一起蜿蜒盘旋，大雨倾盆时，山脉更显挺拔险峻。

峡谷之上，坐落着肇庆古城，它毫不起眼，在名为"七星岩"的7块白色大理石上陡峭险峻的地方，建有很多庙宇。这些庙宇古色古香、精美绝伦，只能攀爬进入其中。主庙在悬崖底部，里面有观音菩萨的铜像，两位护财童子各站一边，这些铜像约10英尺高，据估计已有超过1000年历史了，庙里还有一个年岁更加久远的铜钟。

通过一个大山洞，再沿着大理石石阶而上，就抵达了一座大理石庙宇，里面有一尊天后坐像。修建庙宇和制作塑像都是由岩石雕琢而成的，天后的塑像位于一个洞顶端有开口的神龛内，这样，顶部的自然光线投射到精雕细琢的塑像和白色大理石褶皱上，熠熠生辉。七星岩附近的土地十分平坦，很适合人们种植稻米、荷花，以及养鱼。庙宇脚下的一个大池塘中，一只母水牛

正在撕扯着漂浮在水面上的大荷叶吃，而小牛则平静地跟随在母亲身侧游着，不时将头靠在母亲身上。要明白，水牛对中国经济的影响是举足轻重的，因为如果没有水牛，水稻的耕种就会大打折扣。水牛牵着犁，耕犁水田，田里的泥水漫过它的肚皮，其他的动物根本无法将这样粗糙的犁拖到泥地里。肇庆以其锡制品闻名，七星岩上的各种大理石也可以雕刻成精美的工艺品。

肇庆的西部是广西的梧州城，桂江和西江在该城交汇。以往，桂江上有一座吊桥，现已不存在了，不过如今还有 2 根约 9 英尺高、直径 12 英寸的铁柱仍然矗立在那里，它们已经历了数百年的风霜了。两根铁柱被焊入地里的深度约 4 英尺，我不知道现在铸铁能不能进行焊接，如果不能，那这项中国人熟知的技能就失传了。

沿梧州顺流而下，河岸右侧的一个地区平坦开阔，总有一天会吸引伟大的运动员光临。这里有很多老虎，所以很不安全，下午四五点过后，居民都不敢出门。再向下游走，左岸上有一座中国重要的佛教庙宇——后沥佛寺，这里约有 200 名僧侣，而且还能容纳 200 名香客，香客们在一年中的某些特定时刻前来烧香拜佛禅修。该寺庙位于距离河岸 2 英里远的一座山上，距地平面 1500 英尺高。通往寺庙的山路陡峭，庙门前有两名身穿灰色长袍的和尚守卫，手握长矛以防止不法之徒进入。尽管山路陡峭，然而进入寺庙，却比较平坦，而且附近有一片繁茂的原始森林，更显环境清幽。寺庙的香火旺盛，香客众多，每天都有礼佛的仪式，而且这里跟中国其他地方的寺庙不一样，整洁干净，设备齐全。我参观寺庙的时候，众僧侣和其他信众正在吟诵经文，每一次重复经文的时候，他们都要跪在地上磕头。念诵经文的时候，伴奏的乐器只有锣和鼓，和尚敲打木鱼以控制节奏，不过声音不大。一位和尚要敲击两三种不同大小的锣，最小的一种直径仅有6英寸。平常摆放经文的长桌上摆满了水果和糕点，桌前挂着精美的刺绣。这样一次礼拜的钱由香客们出，香客们享用到桌上的食物，他们也可以带回家跟其他人分享。

随后我跟庙里的方丈进行了一番长谈，他非常和蔼，十分友好。他说出家人也有自己的习俗规则要遵守，就这一点来看，我认为，这座寺庙是一个独立的共同体。寺庙里有多座神龛，每座神龛都有香烛和念珠出售，香火十分旺盛。低处的会客室里有几位女士，在等待的时候她们买了一位和尚所写的祷文。每一份祷文的价格从 60 美分到 1 美元不等。

在旱季和雨季，西江最狭窄河段的水位落差有 40 英尺。水位下降到一定程度，河岸就多出了相当大的一块土壤，非常适宜耕种，而且由于水流常年冲刷，留下了丰富的沉积物。这些土地可不能荒废，因此河流水量减少时，土地上种满了庄稼和蔬菜、桑树等，而这些作物在下一季河流涨水之前就会被收割掉，河流就重新恢复了活力。在一个名为甘竹的地区，养蚕业颇具规模，两边的河岸上都种满了桑树，每年产三季桑叶，每次收割都要留下顶端的六七片叶子。蚕宝宝最初是吃的切碎的桑叶，每天至少要换食两次，很小的幼虫则用一根长羽毛引到新鲜的桑叶处。37 天内，蚕宝宝就开始吐丝，并且会持续吐 7 天。河岸旁有很多看似富庶的城镇，一些城镇里林立着这样的杆子，这些杆子顶部有像倒立的金字塔状的东西，就像桅杆一样，通过了科举考试并获得了官位的人就可以在房前竖起这样的杆子，作为荣誉的象征，所有中国官员的衙门前都有两根这样的杆子。

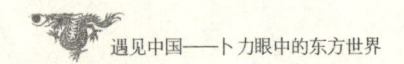

西江当前是通往云南的主要河道,云南和广西西部有大量的牛通过水路送往广东和香港销售。这些商品不时会遭到劫掠,河盗有时也会得到惩罚。城镇的居民只有在同乡遭到了杀害时,才会群起追踪河盗的船,并一直朝盗贼的船开火,直到所有盗贼都被杀死了为止。

第四章

　　西江与长江相比，就是小巫见大巫了，长江承载了中国更大比重的商贸活动。战舰可以从上海的吴淞码头长驱直入，进入距东海边 600 英里远的武汉汉口，长江沿岸自然也有一些海外贸易，但上海是整个长江流域的大外贸中心。长江的历史可透过每年中国海关官员整理的《通商各关华洋贸易全年清册》了解，这是最完整和有趣的统计学资料了。这里记录的一切反映了整个国家的大致情况，只要看一下，商品的供给、需求和价格波动的原因都一目了然。

　　我们读到了一份报道，报道称：国内旱灾之后，发生

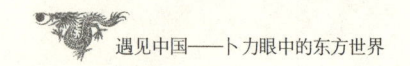

了一次叛变，因此生产受到了影响。叛乱者有1万人左右，用空心的木材制作枪和刀剑等武器。起初，叛军还占据着上风，那些可能还用着旧式兵器的政府"军队"面对着木头枪和刀剑也占不了优势，但2 000名外国士兵加入了政府"军队"，叛军就不堪一击了。在旧中国，用中空的树木做武器是很普遍的。菲律宾起义者反抗西班牙的时候，把木棒换成了铸铁棒，不过还加了铁环作防范。他们还用木头仿制了斯奈德步枪，非常美观，看起来很可怕，不过都不能用来射击。在中国比较偏远的地方，普遍使用的武器仍是抬枪，他们在一系列小型冲突中用这种武器来对抗我们的军队。冲突发生时，我们正在与清政府谈判，我们达成了协议，把九龙地区划为租界归英国管理。抬枪是一种火绳枪，枪管10英尺长，枪口1英寸宽，如果被这种枪的子弹射中，那么伤口就会很严重，不过很多情况下可能会使目标逃过一劫。这种枪需要3个人操纵，2个人要将枪管扛在肩头，第三个人负责开火。枪开火了之后，3位枪手才从开枪时的震颤恢复平静，然后再去重新装载子弹，这道程序可不能心急。快速撤离战场的时候，这种枪反倒成了对方的战利品。与一群人近距离作战，使用大量的抬枪可能很有杀伤力，能够震慑对手，但是，这种摇旗呐喊、短兵相接的英雄时代已经过去了，如今，训练有素的士兵要看枪的准星和射程。

如果有人能够通过中国的海港、河流和小溪去了解我们贸易的方方面面，你们就能看到各种各样的棉、绒、羊毛制品、铜、铁和锡制的器皿、水泥、染料、器械、石油、铁路物资、胡椒、糖、茶末及其他产品，那么他能获取很多有用而有趣的信息。从大船到舢板，从舢板到小船，从小船到独轮手推车、骡子，最后到苦力，这些苦力是唯一能够通过偏远村寨羊肠小道的"工具"，或者在山区的汹涌激流上使用脆弱的运输工具。上文已经提到过，中国的海岸上几乎看不到海藻，但有意思的是，海藻的进口量很大，就跟爱尔兰一样，这些进口的海藻都是用作食物，岩石海藻（红皮藻）和角叉菜薛是常见的品种。这些进口的海洋产品能交换一系列其他商品，如蛋、牛皮（奶牛和水牛的都有）及其他各种兽皮（如驴皮、貂皮等）、丝绸、茶叶、烟草、木材、芝麻和鸦片等，鸦片主要是从陕西、四川和云南运来的，是最重要

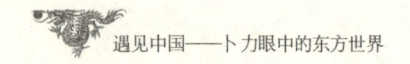

的出口商品之一。我查看了长江港口1906年的年度贸易报告，鸦片的年进口量达到了62 161担，而出口量则达到了643 377担。英国政府是否制定过进口的相关政策，把印度的鸦片出口量每年减少1/10，直到完全不出口，相应地，不仅中国出口的鸦片量会同比下降，其他鸦片种植区也同样会得到控制，人们有兴趣了解这一点。如果没有这样的政策，中国就会再次在应对欧洲人无意间爆发的情感时显示其足智多谋。那些反对鸦片进口的热心人们不时会虔诚地发出抵制鸦片的声明，而且他们通常都怀着力求精确性的热切愿望，然而，他们只看到了笼统的表述，并没有搜集到权威的可靠进出口数据，那些热心人们往往不知不觉带上了强调鸦片危害的强烈感情色彩，并且他们认为自己并未夸大其词。尽管很难系统性地统计出鸦片的实际消费情况，也无法确切地了解鸦片对中国人身心健康的危害究竟有多深，不过在中国香港和新加坡却有可靠的相关调查数据，而某些能人也对中国已知的鸦片消费进行了统计，结果显示，有节制的鸦片吸食对人危害巨大的理论经不起推敲。香港是一个典型的中国城市，这里的人们能够自由吸食鸦片，只要他们能买得起。我现在对香港的中国人的了解，与先前英国政府对这里进行的详尽的调查结果相符，

第四章

中国的劳苦大众很可怜,他们只能通过不断地劳动来养家糊口。一天的工作结束后,那些对鸦片上了瘾的苦力——只占总人口的很小比例,他们走进鸦片店,在那里买回一点点鸦片,然后就躺在长椅或沙发上吸食鸦片,有时候是一个人;有时候则跟朋友一起,分别躺在一盏小灯的两侧,一边谈天说地,一边吸食鸦片。大烟枪的形状很特别,就像一个挖了洞的苹果,他们通过一根烟管从里面吸食。吸食者带着一根像毛衣针那么长的针,从装鸦片膏的盒里取出少量(豌豆大小的)烟丸,然后放到灯盏的火焰上烘烤,直到烟丸烤至适当的黏稠度,再将烟丸放进烟袋锅,在加热过程中烟丸被不断揉捏。然后将烟袋锅放在灯盏的火焰上,深吸并吞咽两三口,烟丸被烧掉了,成了烟灰,再磕掉烟袋锅里的烟灰,以上过程不断重复,直到吸食者变得昏昏欲睡,或者完全麻木,清醒了之后,吸食者就会离开原地。

如果你明白海港城市里的苦力工作多么劳累,你就会知道,这些苦力为什么会吸食鸦片。如果鸦片吸食过量,

显而易见，人们就会变成鸦片上瘾的流浪汉和乞丐，然而事实却恰好相反，因为这世上再没有比中国人更勤劳、更有效率的民族了。

总督任命的委员会近期提交了一份有价值的报告，提出了以下问题：

（1）过度沉迷鸦片现象在英属海峡殖民地的流行程度如何？

（2）上述殖民地鸦片吸食是没节制的还是适度的？

（3）为了根除吸食鸦片对上述殖民地造成的恶劣影响，英国将采取怎样的措施？

委员会里有1位基督教主教，3位立法委员会成员，其中有1名中国人和3位无党派人士。他们调查了75位来自社会各阶层的证人，其中21人是由禁烟的社团推荐的，呈交了一份一共343个段落的报告，我摘录该报告的部分内容如下：

76. 我们确信，中国人养成吸食鸦片恶习的主要原因是因为人本性中的放纵所导致的。

77. 马来半岛的工人阶级与家庭关系淡漠，缺少家庭关爱，工作太过紧张，而且没有健康的休闲方式，这让他们更容易沉迷于鸦片，这种嗜好，无论是它的镇静作用，还是吸食时身体的轻松状态，都让中国人着迷。

91. 调查显示，如果其他条件均不变，对中国人寿保险业务很有经验的人寿保险公司很乐意将那些每天抽两支鸦片烟（116格令①）当作头等的风险，这绝对超出了少量吸食的程度，而我们得知，那些保险公司为这样的风险买单是合情合理的。因此，按照这些评判，吸食鸦片的习惯对寿命并没有太大的影响，我们也没有足够的证据采信相反的观念。

96. 我们按照自己的思维去考虑于我们而言有利的证据，据我们的调查，吸食鸦片造成的恶劣后果通常被放大了。在取证过程中，我们发现，一个中等程度的鸦片吸食者，医生都难以辨别出来，那这些中等程度的鸦片吸食者更难被慈善家们发现，因为光是鸦片依赖程度很重的吸食者已经让他们无比操心。慈善家们对依赖程度很重的人过度关心，并

---

① 格令，重量单位，等于0.064 8克，用于称量药物等。——译者注

且还将他们的状况概括为鸦片吸食者的普遍状况,这无疑也成为夸大鸦片广泛使用带来的恶劣后果的重要原因。

106. 有人指控吸食鸦片会导致人们意识涣散,这一点我们认为未经证实,因为许多大量吸食鸦片的人在事业上都很成功,而且也没有证据显示,吸食鸦片的人无法承担重大的职责。

关于鸦片使用剂量会不断增多的观点,这份报告作出了如下的评论:

112. 此外,我们掌握的诸多具体证据显示,在很长的一段时间内,鸦片使用剂量没有增加,如果以上理论适用于当地鸦片成瘾泛滥的情况,那怎么没有出现本应十分普遍的赤贫现象呢?

关于强制立法禁止吸食鸦片,这份报告是这么说的:

133. 目前，鸦片种植于印度、中国、土耳其和波斯等国，我们认为，如果没有行之有效的普遍禁种措施出台，在一个地区禁种只会导致另一个地区的种植面积扩大。

这份报告接下来还提及了用吗啡代替鸦片，并将之作为最需严肃考虑的问题，使用吗啡比吸食鸦片的危害更大。

近期，上海举行了一次国际委员会会议，会议将如何处理鸦片问题，我们将拭目以待。清朝政府颁布了严苛法令，明令减少鸦片种植，并禁止人们吸食鸦片，而中国人却习惯将与他们的习俗相冲突的诏令看作难以实现的愿望。如果这个法令成功实施，那它所引发的变革将是清朝统治者要求汉人剃发留辫以来最为彻底的。

近年来，各国在中国的贸易额比重表明，英国的贸易量缩减了不少，而德国的贸易量却有所增加，尽管这对英国货运量是一种损失，但对于商品本身来说，商品供应的变化并没有表面上那么明显。近半个多世纪以来，德国获得的大量棉花和其他商品，都是通过英国公司采购，从英国港口运到中国来的。但随着《商标法》的实施，很快情况就发生了改变。精明的中国商人见自己的棉衣上印着广告语,称是产自德国,于是去咨询德国总领事,并称直接跟德国制造商做生意要更好,而精明的中国商人也确实这样做了。随着与中国贸易的兴盛,同样精明的德国人也认为,自己的商品最好是自己派船销售到海外,这样可以节省运送到英国的中转开支,这样,德国对东方的货运量自然也就大幅增加,而且,随着德国大商船的增加,自然就产生了创建海军确保商船安全的提议。因此,大家都非常欣赏的《商标法》变成了英国给德国所做的最大也是最有价值的广告,德国人的技术、做事的周密性以及经营能力全都派上了用场。10年前,香港港口见到的德国旗帜相对比较少,而如今,进出香港港口的德国船的数量已经超过了英国船。

中国的城乡生活差距比欧洲更甚,因为在农村缺乏安全防护,所有的富人都搬到有城墙的城镇生活。长江以南的大城市格局都差不多,社会生活也没有什么不同。城市外围都是25英尺的高墙围绕,墙顶端每隔15到20英尺有方塔

第四章

间隔，东南西北4个方位都有大门。杭州城的北大门是京杭大运河的终点，这是我在中国见过的最美的地方。8块巨石支撑着一栋精美的3层建筑，而顶部收窄为像一艘船一样构造，装饰精美，雕梁画栋。石头建筑的每一个部分都经过了精雕细琢，上半部分还有穿孔。雕刻作品非常精致，人物傲然伫立，花和叶子都是凸雕的，这样枝干才可从它们后方穿过。南京和苏州的城墙周长均为36英里，而城墙内侧还有大量的空地没有建筑物。这些空地可能都是为种植农作物而留的，有了这些作物，在城墙遭遇围攻时，内部的居民还可以用它们果腹以对抗敌军的围攻。这些古老城市中的许多精美的建筑，有的消失了踪迹，有的成了一片废墟。不过随处可见的瓷瓦屋顶，呈现美丽的弧形，铺着绿色或黄色的搪瓷釉瓦，熠熠生辉，这样的设计仍然向我们展示着中国人天生的艺术才华。

南京的明孝陵，1英里长的过道两旁摆放了两排大象、骆驼、石鳌和马等动物的塑像，每座塑像10.5英尺高，都是用一块石头雕刻而成的，跟以前点缀在北京城门上那些巨大的青铜天文仪器不同，这些塑像没有人能够搬走。每头大象的背上都有一叠石头，每一个中国人，经过这里时就会对着它们求财或求子，就像是某种宗教仪式一样。他们会抛起一块石头，如果石头落在象背上，那么他的生活就会美好如意，如果石头落了地，他还是继续生活，也许有悲伤，但也不是完全看不到希望。南京的琉璃塔已经不复存在了，不过琉璃塔上直径15英尺的青铜顶却仍然还在。

城墙内的街道狭窄，有的地方非常肮脏，臭不可闻，虽然我们觉得这气味让人难以忍受，不过中国人显然已经习惯了。从卫生的角度而言，这种气味比下水道的臭味要好一点，尽管这种气味不能定义为"脏"，但显然不应该是公共场所中出现的。

北京跟南方的任何城市都不一样。北京的街道宽阔，北方不同民族的混杂为街头风貌增加了多样性和色彩。街道上会遇到从蒙古驮着货物来的骆驼长队，它们跟随着主人的驼铃前行，不时咕哝抱怨着。北京的马车有着装饰华丽的车轮，但没有缓冲装置，当马车驶过宽阔而肮脏的街道上突起的地方，冬日的泥浆和夏日的尘土能减轻这精致但不舒服的车辆的颠簸。有时候，马车里坐着妆容精致的女士，她们身旁有大量的侍从跟随。偶尔也会见到涂着红色油漆的镀金大棺材，被搁置在一个大竹架子上，这个架子通常需要20到五六十人来抬。如果是一位大臣下葬，那么抬棺材的人可能多达100位，这种壮观的场面在南方城市的狭窄街道上是看不到的。北京分为4个城区，外围有巨大的城墙包围，城墙50英尺高，城墙顶端可能有三四十英尺宽。一些公使就是在城墙的这一部分指挥了某些最艰难的围攻战斗。

先农坛和天坛分别位于北京外墙南大门的左右两侧。两座神坛各坐落于一座公园中，中国农历新年的第一天，皇帝会在天坛的白色大理石平台上祭祀，为所统治的臣民祈福。然后，在立春的时候，皇帝会依照古时传下的惯例，率众大臣去先农坛举行祭祀仪式。纪念开春的仪式是这一年中最为重要的事情之一，皇帝率众臣来到先农坛，庄重地犁出一道沟；牵引犁的水牛用月季和其他鲜花装饰，犁也要用象征着皇家尊荣的金黄色丝绸覆盖；土地已经被耕得很松软了，不过留出一条坚硬的小路供皇帝犁地时行走，犁地前，皇帝褪去了华丽的龙袍，将长长的丝质衣物缠绕在腰间，就像木匠把围裙掀起，解放双腿一样。皇帝犁完了之后，3位皇子也各牵着一条水牛，赶着一架用红色丝绸装饰的犁，每人犁出三道沟，随后是9位主要官员，他们所用的牛和犁的装饰也跟那些皇子们的是一样的。然后，他们会种下一种称作"红莲"的米，到收获时，这种谷物会被当作祭品——其中一半被送往神农庙的祭坛，另一半则供奉在王室的宗祠中的牌位前。

这种仪式是从远古时代流传下来的，它表现了中国人对农业生产的重视。在大约成书于公元前1000年的周朝典籍中，关于反对骄奢淫逸，书中是这样说的："文王卑服，即康功田功。"（语出《尚书·无逸》）

北京是中国的仕途生活中心，因此一直都有很多官吏聚集在这里，每一位高级官员——总督、州府台，或称道台，以及其他低级别官员——都要在自己任期结束时对自己的管理工作作一个总结，并申请连任。如果3年的任期内，一位总督获得了300万美元，如果希望见到皇上、谋求续任，他至少要向宫中各级官员送出100万美元的礼金。许多官员动用积蓄购买瓷器，而不是将它们用于投资或储存。某些瓷器会被埋在地下或藏在某个安全的地方，如果主人需要钱用，就会卖掉一件。在英国，人们普遍认为，英国市面上那些值钱的瓷器在中国的任何城镇中都能买到，这是错误的观点。当然，任何地方都可能买到物超所值的瓷器，然而品质优良的瓷器在中国跟在欧洲一样昂贵，北京的一位古玩行家给我看了一个非常漂亮的瓷花瓶，他开价为1.7万美元。中国人将购买瓷器作为储蓄银行投资并在需要钱的时候重新售出，这种习惯的结果就是高品质的瓷器持续流通，而且通常都是按原始价格出售的。

第 五 章

中国农民耕种者的一生是在间歇性辛勤劳动中度过的。北方只有一年产一季的作物，而南方才有一年产两季的作物。主要的作物是大米，农民必然要选择与人合作，这一片地与那一片地之间没有围栏，好像所有水稻都是种在一大片平坦的土地上，有时被细分为一个个小块，所有稻谷要在同一时间收割。稻谷收割了之后，在洪水将这些田地淹没之前，这些田地就变成了牛儿的牧场，这个阶段也为种植下一季作物做准备。

农民若是播种迟了，那就必须找到一种生长速度更快的作物种子，某种稻米从播种到成熟所需的时间，可能要比别的种类的少一个多月。但即使种子已经下种并长起来了，过道或者沟渠边的草也不能浪费，小孩子坐在牛背上，来到田间地头，让牛吃过道或沟渠边的草，同时还要阻止它们食用长出的作物。

南方的第一季水稻约在4月时播种，7月上旬收割，第二季水稻在7月末播种，9月末收割。每季播种前，田地都要重新翻一次，当在苗圃里被种得密密麻麻的稻苗被移植到水田地里并在此生根发芽后，每棵植株脚下都堆满了泥土。水稻长到1英尺高时，就施一次猪粪肥，就是猪粪里掺杂着石灰和泥土，水位低的时候用手撒在田里。如果作物看起来长势不好，那么肥料就会仔细播撒到每一棵植株旁，如果植株的长势还是不好，那就要把肥料兑上水，让肥料化开，呈液体状，再浇到植株旁。稻田里的水一直要保存到收割之前的一段时间，谷物完全成熟，抽穗之后，中国人希望降3天雨，他们认为这样会增加很多产量。

水稻植株长到水面上6—8英寸高的时候，田地里的水深约3英寸，大量的鸭和鹅会来稻田里吃青蛙以及其他昆虫（大米去除稻壳之前称为"稻"），一位成年男士或男孩，手持一根长竹竿,竹竿顶端绑有一束竹叶,赶着它们过来。傍晚的时候,赶鸭人只要摇一摇竹竿,所有的鸭子或鹅都会离开田地,这些家禽数量可多达上百只,落在最后的鸭或鹅会挨竹竿抽。鸭和鹅训练久了,一旦看到主人摇竹竿,就会用最快的速度摇摇摆摆向前冲刺,以免落到最后,这样的场景真是有趣。一旦到了地上,这群家禽就走在前方了,主人将竹竿搁在岸边,所有的家禽跳过去,主人则计数。中国南方饲养的鸭子数量惊人,鸭蛋都是在发酵的稻谷壳堆上孵化的。每家乡村店铺都有一些腊鸭,鸭子都被切割成两半,然后压扁。任何动物都可以用作食材,老鼠也用同样的方式风干并售卖,但家鼠在餐桌上并不常见,用于售卖的都是在稻田里发现的田鼠。除了稻谷,农夫还种植油菜、水果以及其他各种蔬菜。在丝绸产区,桑树是主要的种植作物,而长江沿岸盛产茶叶,西部的大部分地区都在种植罂粟。中国农村跟爱尔兰农村一样,猪是其中很重要的经济支柱,因为猪就是个"储蓄罐",残羹剩饭都可以喂给它吃。中国的猪一般是黑色的,背部奇怪地凹进去,肚子几乎垂到地面上,很容易养肥。通常,烤乳猪都是筵席上的一道主菜。

中国农民生性节俭,不过喜欢玩牌消遣,也喜欢玩各种中国人独创的赌博游戏。喜欢斗鸡或蟋蟀,斗蟋蟀的时候,围观的人数量可达数千。人们建一个大草棚,蟋蟀坑就在其中,斗蟋蟀的真正场所是一个圆圆的碗,底部平坦,直径约7英寸,两只蟋蟀被放入碗中,人们用一根小长棍,如笔杆,拴上老鼠毛,轻轻搔弄蟋蟀背部,使其感觉痒而变得激动起来。受到刺激的两只蟋蟀则展开了一场大战,直到其中一只打输了掉头逃跑为止。这样的竞赛举行时,人们会为上场的蟋蟀下大笔赌注,群情激奋。如果有人足够幸运,捕获了一只好斗的蟋蟀,那他就会给它准备特别的大餐。出名的蟋蟀有时候会被转手好几次,而且价格不菲。毕竟,这种蟋蟀,就像赛马一样,是以其获胜的能力而获得高价的。最初,获得蟋蟀的代价就是要费精力去抓它,这种

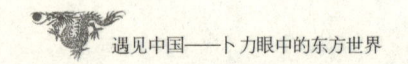

娱乐方式最贫苦的穷人也可以去享受，而村民用钱币（一美分的十分之一）赌博时的兴奋情绪不亚于富裕的城里人花高价下赌注时的感觉。

　　农夫的家里家具摆设并不奢华，但却足以满足他的需要。除了桌子，其他的一切几乎都是用竹子制作的，只要有水火，竹子可以被弯曲成任何形状，灯具则分陶、锡和黄铜等数种，黄铜灯具跟古代罗马的灯具形状差不多。床就是一块朴素的平木板，上面铺着草席或棕榈叶席子，枕头则是一块半圆柱形的陶器，长约10英寸，高4英寸，通常被做成一个靠双手和膝盖支撑身体的人形，人形背部则是枕头的主体。细心的家庭主妇将针线活儿放在里面，这"枕头"就变成了好用的针线袋。冬天，这个陶制的枕头被替换一个软皮革的枕头，这样就不会太冷。南方农夫家门旁边有一个蜂箱，就是由竹子做的鼓状物，长2英尺，直径12英寸，平时以干黏土覆盖。农夫的耕种工具——一把锄头，一个木制的犁，大约跟古埃及遗迹中的工具差不多形状，出去劳作的时候，农夫将工具扛在肩上，赶到田地里；还有一个木制的平板状"耙子"，用以锄松种植水稻的土壤——被放置在房间的角落里。农夫的打扮大都不很整洁，并且对身上的虫子不屑一顾。但有时候,农夫也会沉溺于在自己身上设"陷阱",捉跳蚤,用一根直径3英寸的竹节,将两头削去,仅留其中一小节,将这一段竹节放在袖子里,不过他们放了什么作为诱饵,我还没看到过。

除了赌博,农夫每年收割季节前后还要去寺庙里拜佛,还要参加婚葬礼,加入游行队伍,还会去中国的七大圣山之一参拜。农夫通常只有一个妻子,她完全听从他的摆布,并且对他的管理非常严格,丈夫就是她的法律,丈夫为家庭宗法的情感中心。她必须全心全力照顾孩子,她总是会担心迷信中的恶魔现身,降临到自家的儿子身上,给家庭带来厄运。为此她会将男孩打扮成女孩的模样,她总是担心这骗不过那些最蠢笨的恶魔。她还不能忽略了宗教职责,因此她经常去寺庙里虔心祈祷,然后在神像前的祭坛上拿过两块肾脏形状的木头,一头扁平一头圆,她将扁平的一头握在手中,然后将木片向上抛,观察它们掉落的方向,如果两块都是扁平状的向上,那这就表示好运,如果都是圆头向上,那就表示厄运,如果一根是扁平向上，一根圆头向上，那就是没有答案。她要重复抛掷3次，或者去取一个竹筒，竹筒里有一些写着数字的签，她摇晃竹筒，就像内斯特摇晃着阿伽门农的头盔那样，直到里边掉出来一个，她就会按照这个掉出来的数字去房间里的墙壁上取一张标有相同数字的黄纸，这纸上写着的是对她的祷告的神秘回答。

  一个临时的调查者是很难理解中国人的宗教信仰的。在很多方面，他们都是非常切实的，他们有着执着的信仰，至少体现在他们相信有重生和来世，尽管他们的精神状态更多的是一种对恶魔的恐惧，而不是对仁慈的神的信仰，但他们对接受的恩惠抱有敬畏和谢意。某天，在珠江沿岸的开元寺——这家寺院很华丽很舒适——我看到一个渔夫和他的家人带着一篮子鱼和水果进了寺里，他将这些东西都放到祭坛上，随后他击鼓一次，好像是要让神明注意，家人们虔诚祈祷，而这位渔夫将酒洒在祭坛上7次。我问方丈，这种行为有什么含义，他回答说，这位先生前一天晚上捕了很多鱼，因此他携家人过来谢恩。有时候，家人病了，他们也会到寺庙里来，请和尚在纸上写下一段祷文，然后将纸烧掉，他们将烧完的灰烬带回家里，把它们当作药物服下。还是在广州的一家寺庙里，我看到一根柱子上挂满了纸片人，而且是倒挂着的。我又问这是什么意思，得到的回答是，这些纸片人是某些女人用来诅咒男人的，那些男人抛弃了她们，回家娶妻生子，在这一点上，中国跟西方文明的中心都是一样的。被抛弃的女人希望这些咒语，以及被粘贴在柱子上的人形，能够逼迫她们的相好回到自己身边，不过显然，这样是行不通的。

每年每个地区都有戏剧表演，通常最让农民兴奋的就是这些表演，戏班子会搭建自己的剧场，就是一个能容纳1000名观众的露天剧场。这个剧场几天之内就能建好，一个礼拜左右的时间里，各种历史剧和社会剧会在这里上演。演员要经过化妆和穿特制的戏服才能上台表演，有时候，观众中的知名人士也会上台。所有的演员都是男性，因为女人不能抛头露面，不能出来唱戏，然而男演员扮演的女人非常逼真，而且其中有些演员的酬劳很高。戏服都非常精美。在历史剧中，所有演员都要戴上很长很厚的胡须，完全将嘴巴盖住了。剧中的坏人很容易区分，因为坏人的脸都被涂成了黑色，鼻子上还有一个白色的点。整部剧是以唱的形式表达的，演员按照一种简单而不断重复的节奏，唱出自己的台词，旁边还有几种奇形怪状的弦类乐器伴奏，当剧情进入关键部分，或者到冲突爆发的时候，伴奏者就会敲击铙钹，发出震耳欲聋的声音，人物唱念台词的时候则没有这种声音。道具都放在台上的一个大箱子里。如果演员正要过桥，那么舞台上灵活机动的工作人员就会在舞台两边各放一张桌子和一把椅子，并在桌椅上盖上一块布，这就是所谓的"桥"。演员走过去了之后，桌椅就被撤掉了。如果演员要骑马或者坐上一把椅子，也有惯例性的动作传达给观众。

战争中总有个人会被杀害，工作人员走上前来，用一卷白纸或白布遮盖住被害的人，此时被害的人则自己起身离开。而在日本，这种剧情的安排又跟中国不同。在日本的戏剧中，总有两个身着黑色水袖衣服的人，这两个人观众们是当他们看不见的。如果剧中有人被害了，那么这两人中的一个站在"被害人"前方，伸开双臂，"被害"的人离开舞台，"看不见的人"跟在他身后，将他和其他观众隔离开来。

在社会剧中，演员的服装就没有历史剧中那么奢华精美了，而是穿着现当代的服装。如果演员扮演的是穷人,那他就会用手指做出掸掉衣服上的虱子跳蚤等寄生虫的动作。

观众对台上的演出异常感兴趣,都目不转睛地盯着舞台,有时候看到悲伤的剧情还会流出眼泪来。

在中国的社会中,演员的地位是非常低的,演员及其子女都不能参加科举考试,悲喜剧演员是一个非常庞大的群体。

演出结束时,如果有富人在场,他们的仆人就会将一串串铜钱扔到舞台上,这些钱就是演员的酬劳。

但是,只有风调雨顺的年份里才会唱戏。干旱少雨的季节,河流水位很低,稻米产量锐减,那么这些地区就会遭遇饥荒,人们不满的情绪以及对生活的无望感会导致当地严重的动乱,人们会将这次饥荒当作是统治者惹怒了上天,失去了神明的信任的象征,而统治者的代表就是当地的官员。人们有了这种想法,就会起来造反,而这种造反的苗头一旦被政府发现,那政府就会用令人恐惧的手段去对付造反的人。

1903年,广西省爆发了一场饥荒,饥荒过程中爆发了一场暴乱。这场暴乱的令人痛心的描述传到了香港,很快香港就建立了救援会,救援会派出一名官员去广西了解相

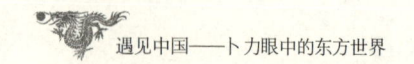

关情况，官员回来时便就他所见到的情况作了汇报。广西省爆发了一场叛乱，镇压叛乱时逮捕了很多人。这些不幸的人其中大部分人是罪犯，都被处决，监狱中犯人的提审也受到了影响，治安官称，普通的老百姓都没有食物，那么，囚犯就更没有吃的了，只好把他们处死。饿死的人数逐日增加，人们甚至相易而食。与此同时，权贵们都在尽力减轻人们的痛苦，不过大家都太贫困了，征不到税。香港救援会的代表，带上了第一批救援用的大米，达到了广西，当地的官员就为他提供了所有便利设施，不仅提供了警卫，还派了一艘汽艇拖着运粮食的舢板船过河。当地官员派给这个代表的警卫还跟他讲了一个故事，从这个故事中可看出当地的社会已沦落到多么残忍的地步。不久前，当地官员得知了一个盗贼团伙的驻扎地，当地官员派遣军队，也包括讲述故事的警卫，一起去了那个村庄，并抓获了盗贼团伙的所有人。他们将一个男盗贼的腹部切开，取出内脏，并当着奄奄一息的受害者的面，烹煮并食用他们的内脏。他们还砍掉了女人的胸部，也烹煮并食用了它们。那名警卫说，被砍掉了胸部的女人整个过程中都在啜泣，随后，这两人被杀害了。由于那些"将士"们不愿意自己杀害孩子，因此他们将刀交给周围的孩子，让他们杀掉那

第五章

些小孩子。

这个故事骇人听闻，不过这样的结局显示了，即使在中国，无论意图多么高尚，专制权力都有着过度残暴实施的潜在危险。灾荒发生后，广西当地官员一直在努力应对饥荒，但叛乱火上浇油，政府的军队在交战过程中并没有占上风。香港和广州的救援会将大米运到饥荒区，当地的主政官员是一位有教养的绅士，他非常同情灾区的人民，因此也尽力给予了救援会所需要的帮助。他对待香港救援会工作人员的态度一直都是彬彬有礼的，而且参与物资分配的工作人员在行动结束后都受到了恰如其分的感谢，不过工作人员对那位官员的谢意却没传到他的耳朵里。广州的新任总督上任了，上任之后就去了饥荒区做私下调查，他发现那名官员处事并不公正，而且将无辜民众当罪犯处死，还处死了总督秘密派遣去调查真实情况的一名调查员。发现了这件事之后，总督贬黜了那名官员，官员因此而自杀。读到这里，大家都会对这种草菅人命的行为大吃一惊，在总督介入调查前这位官员未被人毒死真是令人诧异，毒药大家并不陌生，制作这种毒药的植物在中国被称作马通。它无色无味，但如果泡茶的时候加一点点，人几乎是必死无疑的。

东西方文化发生碰撞的海岸城市里，生活是极富乐趣的。每个通商口岸都有外国租界，租界领事具有绝对的统治权，而且还有完全西方化的警力机构和政管机构。天津、上海、宁波、福州、厦门、广州，以及长江各港口城市周边地区，都有大量中国政府失去主权的地方。这些地方，所有犯罪案件和争端都是欧洲国家法官和领事法庭来审理，上海除外，在这里，某些犯罪案件则需要欧洲国家法官和中国法官共同审理。在上海这座城市里，外国租界与中国城市形成了强烈反差：租界这边有豪华的外滩码头，精心打理的公共花园，还有优秀的警力人员（骑马的和徒步的），宽敞的街道两旁，展示欧洲新款式的精美店铺林立，供租赁的马车停靠在指定的街角，等待着雇主，这些马车装备精良，但价格还算合理，而贫穷的中国人则普遍使用独轮手推车——这种车弥尔顿曾在作品中提到过——爱尔兰的双轮敞篷马车，可能就是以这种车为原型而设计出来的。这种车的车轴位于车体的正中央，巨大的车轮上是一个木制的井字形架子，架子两侧各有一个座位。人坐上去抬起腿以后，推车的把手处就没有重量压着了，因此车夫只需要保持车体平衡，并拉车前行。这种推车在长江流域随处可见，并且很适合将沉重的货物运过非常狭窄的、不适合双轮车通行的过道。在上海，这种车不只是用于运送沉重的货物，那些喜欢乘车而不爱步行的中国平民也经常乘坐这种车出行。早晚上下班时间，一个车夫可能要送6个人出行，每侧各坐3人，有时候，一侧坐着1—2个人，而另一侧则是一头猪。

　　沿着河岸往前行，外滩延伸，离开了租界，进入华界，在警力安排上还能见到西方影响，殖民地的中国警察跟外国派驻警察穿着同样的服装。然而华界围墙内的景致却不一样，这里的城市不繁华，也不干净，是中国最为肮脏的地方之一。但是这里的大寺庙附近倒是景色秀美,让人印象深刻。上海市郊的平地上通常是墓地,按照这里丧葬的风俗,棺材要放置到地面上,坟墓有的用砖头建造,有的棺材上仅仅覆盖着茅草,还有的棺材直接放置在地面上,什么覆盖遮掩物都没有。必须要提一句,中国的棺材非常结实,形状很奇特,是用很厚实的木板做成的。每个方位都有桃园,开花的时候,就形成一道像日本的樱花一样美丽的景观。整个长江口平原区沟壑纵横,上海捕猎者俱乐部的成员,不时要踏进这泥泞的沟壑底部捕猎。上海位于长江入海口处,注定要成为中国中部未来的商贸中心,中部18个省份有9个省份的商贸进出都是通过这里。中外群体的社交受到严格限制,不过限令在双方地区都没有得到完全实施,但是,如果贸易关系也受到限制,租界内外就无法和谐相处,那么双方的分歧就会愈加明显,中国这"沉睡的雄狮"明亮的眼睛已经完全打开了,并已经明白有能力和权力根据自己的需求坚持与世界各大强国互惠互利的原则。

第五章

对外国人而言，最令人印象深刻的中国城市是广州，这里人口众多，极富活力。厦门城的外国租界位于珠江岸边，租界另一侧是一条运河，通往租界的唯一通道就是两座戒备森严的桥。租界里的一切都是西式的——西式的建筑、草坪，西式的运动会；各国领事馆前都飘扬着各自的旗帜；看惯了河上来来回回的船只，转身去看租界，若不是租界里还有中国人出入，人们还会以为这里是富庶的欧洲城市郊区。不过，一旦过了桥，经过了那些商铺——曾经这些商铺都是欧洲国家商行的仓库——欧式的风格就完全消失了，映入眼帘的是古老的中式城区，城中景象在中国已存在了几个世纪。街道的宽度从 6—10 英尺不等，全都铺着花岗岩石板，狭窄的街道上来来往往的都是穿着蓝色长袍的中国人，所有人都为自己的事情而奔忙，但如果有外国人进入店铺买东西，那就会引来一群人好奇地驻足观望。街道原本就狭窄，两旁的店铺还在外面挂出色彩斑斓的广告牌，有的广告牌上甚至还有镀金的文字，就更显得空间逼仄。有的广告牌长度 10—12 英尺，而且每种不同的商铺广告牌都有自己特定的色彩和形状。五彩斑斓的广告牌、商店里琳琅满目的商品，还有挂在各家门前喜庆的灯笼，无一不透露出人们生活的富裕程度和艺术气息。

各家店铺一大早就开门，因为店铺内通常没有橱窗，商品都是在柜台上等待出售，各种商贸活动都在这里开展，因此来这里就像是逛一个巨大的集市。不同的生意占据的地方不一样，所以一个商店或一排店铺可能出售昂贵的丝绸和其他东西，所以可能街道这一段的店铺里都是华美的商品，但挨着它的另一段却是屠夫和渔贩的案板，这种突然的转变随处可见，根本不符合我们的搭配观。制作扇子的店铺里，工人们正在忙着制作精美的扇子，广州城就是以这种扇子扬名在外。有的店铺则是制作并修补鞋帽的。裁缝、制袜匠、木匠和铁匠都在勤奋工作，到处都有工匠们在对着珠宝、黄铜或丝绸制品沉思。而羽毛匠们正用翠鸟鲜艳的羽毛制作精美的纹案图形，这种工作非常精细，因此只有年轻人才能做，而且极考验人的视力，年轻的工匠也只能做两年。街角的茶馆，从地面到屋檐都经过了精心装饰和雕琢，闪耀着灿烂的光芒。玉器店和瓷器店里，象牙刀在精雕细刻，摆设的商品精美。许多街道上还有鸟店，店里的鸟儿有的很会唱歌，有的羽毛艳丽，深得中国人喜爱，有的中国富人甚至为自己的爱鸟花巨资打造象牙鸟笼。偏僻的小巷中是很难见到这些商铺的，这里是粗俗的生意店铺的天下——如屠夫、渔民和菜农等。这些巷道中的气味欧洲人很难忍受,中国人却好像普遍都能接受,不过对气味的喜好和厌恶或许不仅仅是个人的特性,而牵涉到一个民族。对我们来说,麝香令一些人愉悦,也令一些人厌恶。

中国城市尽管街道非常狭窄,不适合车辆通行,但街道上仍然很热闹、喧嚣,货郎背着大篮,篮子里装满货物或蔬菜,边走边朝人们大声吆喝,所有人遇到他们都必须让路。街道上不时有官员骑马或乘坐轿辇经过,一大批仆人尾随其后,所有平民百姓都自觉为他让路,让他畅通无阻。显而易见,人们认可这种几乎专制的权力,而这种权力也标示出实际的民主社会中官员的特殊地位。第一次走上这种熙熙攘攘的狭窄街道的陌生人,通常都会望而生畏,感觉就像进入了一个人群蚁冢中的迷宫,如果有暴行发生,人

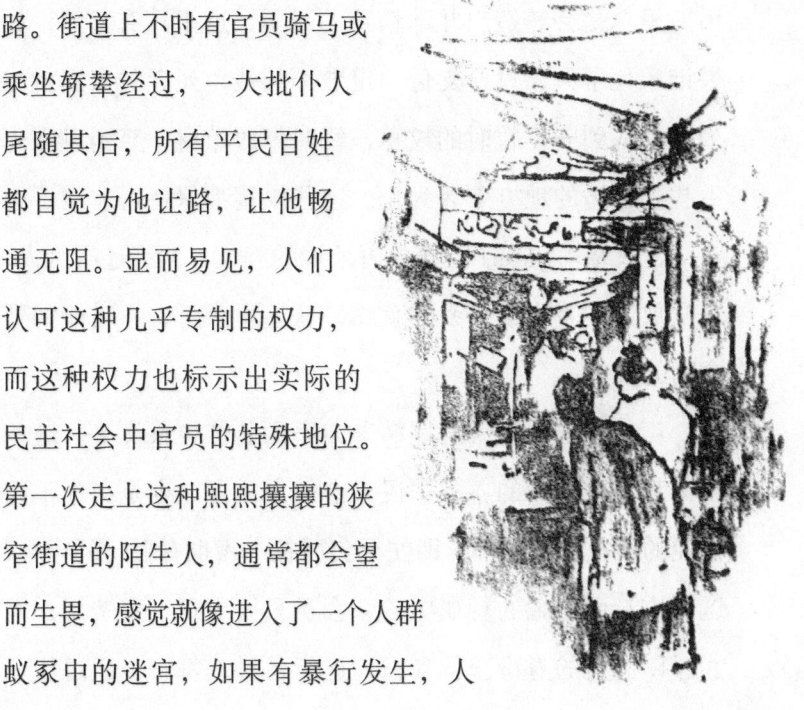

是无法逃脱的。不过广州城的有趣之处丝毫没有因拥挤的街道而耗尽——虽然人力车占据了街道一半的路面,但却从不乱撞——但是,好玩的地方不在拥挤的街道上,这里有被人翻来覆去描述的寺庙,还有6个多世纪一直未曾停止过的水钟;政府的铸币厂里总是会铸造出并不精致的钱币,这里还有墓园,如果谁家死了人,只要支付一定数额的钱,死者的家属就能为死者买到一座暂时的坟墓,暂时停放棺材,直到风水先生找到合适的地方下葬为止。这些坟墓都保持得非常干净整洁,坟墓前的桌子上摆放着死者的牌位,两旁还有纸人,还摆放着死者生前最爱的食物,从这里经过,不时能闻到食物的香气。

广州城里的会馆房屋精美,室内装饰也很漂亮。这些会馆都是在广州的各省居民聚会的俱乐部,也是当地不同行业的成员的俱乐部。即便是乞丐在广州也有自己的行会,这一古老而荣耀的行业中的新会员只要支付一定费用,就能够以会员的身份获得食宿,进行乞讨。每一个通过认证

第五章

的乞丐都携带一个标志物，这标志着他有权进入商铺要求得到救济。

1900年，两江总督刘坤一从北京回南京时，随行人员中就有乞丐帮的首领。首领身着乞丐最为华丽的衣服，跟其他官员们一样有地位，而且也携带着自己的随从和军队。乞丐帮的首领也乘坐轿辇，身边跟随着不同寻常、形形色色的乞丐队伍，他们也都穿着普通的衣物。如果再配上什么武器，他们可能跟福斯塔夫[①]的褴褛衣团差不多了。每家店铺每天至少会迎来一名乞丐光顾，无论是按法律规定还是按风俗习惯，店主都要给乞丐一点接济。这很可能是户外救济的一种形式，如果我们能够明白这种形式的内在运行机制，那么焦虑的英国社会调研者也能学会这种方式以解决国内的难题。

如果店主拒绝进行习以为常的施舍，他可能会发现一名患有可怕疾病的乞丐坐在店门前，他会一直待到店主给予捐赠满足行业需求为止，没有执法严厉的警察，来命令坚持不懈的乞丐离开。我所见过的最令人痛苦的情景是，

[①] 福斯塔夫，莎士比亚历史剧中的人物，他自私、懒惰、畏缩，却又机警、灵巧、乐观。——译者注

在九龙新区，一个很深的沼泽中间的一小块干燥的土地被划给了一群麻风病人。而通往这个干燥地方的唯一通道就是架在沼泽上的一条小径。他们在这块空地上用木箱子的木片建造了简陋的房舍，雨水很轻易就能渗透进去。每天早晨，这些悲惨的人都会去临近的村庄里行乞，而好心的村民会将米饭摆放到自家门前供他们前来食用，我从未见过比他们更加悲惨的人。我在那片沼泽附近为他们建造了更宽敞、更适合他们居住的房屋，这样能给他们遮风挡雨，他们也不用担心房屋被洪水冲毁。广州城里还有一家治疗麻风病的正规专业医院。

但我们并不能说，广州完全是一座零售业城市，因为这里还有很多重要的工厂，有的厂房占据了很大的面积，而且厂里有很多不同工种的工人。这座城市的商贸部门十分拥挤，有人好奇这里是否会被火灾夷为平地，但是，城里的每家店铺的屋顶上都储存了水，以防万一。土地的价格很高，每平方英尺土地的平均价格是14美元，约合每英亩6万英镑。如果有外国高官拜会两广总督，那么广州狭窄的街道上的景象就颇为壮观了。所有的街道上都有士兵把守，他们在街道一侧站成很长一排——因为街道太狭窄了，无法容纳两列军队——每人都携带着自己的旗帜，另一侧则是密集的群众，他们都挤到了店铺的屋檐下，站在那里静静观看官员们的轿辇经过。街道不仅经过了打扫，还经过了清洗，要确保绝对干净。每一个城门前都有6个人手持长喇叭，就像是文艺复兴时期的著名画家弗拉·安杰利科画的吹奏着颂歌的天使一样，这些人会吹奏出两种很长的音调，一种很高，一种很低。总督衙门的院子里有一个约150人的特别护卫队，身着华贵的衣服，手持武器，就像是人们在中国古典画作中所见到的那样——手柄很长的大弯刀、三叉戟，等等——还有三四十人持着紫色、黄色、蓝色或红色的丝绸旗帜，每一面旗帜的面积约12平方英尺，旗杆至少20英尺高，这种场面真是相当壮观。衙门外有两个大型的公园，其中一个里面有很多好木材，另一个曾经被划入了英国领事馆，不过现在被海峡殖民地和香港的实习军官使用了，这些实习军官到殖民地任职前，要先去广州学两年中文。

中国的高官工作很忙碌，不过他的工作环境还是比较安静的。官员们不会听到纷繁的街道上杂乱的噪声，城里的街道太过狭窄，不适合大车通行，所以也听不到机车的轰鸣，感受不到车辆经过时所产生的震颤感。衙门和办公场所与喧闹的街区是分隔开来的，但是衙门里发生的事外面的民众都能知晓。衙门的"差役"，也就是那些随从和信使，主管着衙门里的工作。审案时，只有在掌刑者和其他人证在场的情况下，官员才能提审犯人，不可向好奇的局外者透露消息，这样就保持了审案的神圣性和神秘感。如果没有关于外国人的案件，也许就没有那么多急切的打探者。只要你感兴趣，衙门里的事几乎都可以打听到。

官员是根据以往的惯例来处理日常工作的，无论他多么精力充沛，他都要确保在工作中不作出过多的改变，他也不会轻率地偏离常规。通常，政府或官员的不作为，无论受到多少抨击，都不会引起人们的公愤。在中国，政府高官唯一要担心的就是被派往各地的督察官员向更上级揭发，他们甚至敢于检举最高官员的渎职以及收取佣金等行为，从而证实了中国也有官员像其他民族和国家的官员一样无畏和独立,我们都是在歌曲和故事中听说这些官员的尊姓大名的。

中国人十分注重礼仪,所有的公众场合都很讲究秩序,一个有教养的中国人是不能有粗俗的言语和行为的。中国的文字有多种不同的解读,在跟中国政府签和约时,通常使用3种文字,包括中文、法文和英文,以及其他缔约国的文字,而且总是规定,解读和约条款时,需要用法文或英文而不是用中文去解读条款的确切内容。这并不是说,用中文解读怕中国人耍诈,而是因为中国的许多单个的汉字有多种不同的含义,而真正的含义有时需通过语境来推断,因此同样的条款可能被解读出不同的含义来,那么人们就很难理解到和约条款的确切含义。人们普遍认为,罗伯特·赫德和柏卓安是唯一掌握了中文书写艺术的外国人,他们能够辨认和约的中文表达是否准确。因为这里没有多层的房子,中国高层官员的办公场所和生活居所占地面积都很大。如果房屋很高,就与中国人所信仰的风水相冲突,带来灾难,而且会遭到人们的怨恨。外国人在中国建的教堂的尖顶曾让中国人的敌对情绪逐日高涨,中国人每天都在诅咒,但是教堂还是存在下来了,但中国人并不是默许了教堂的存在,只是耐心忍受这种屈辱,如果他们对教堂

还存有迷信的话,那么这种迷信就是教堂向他们传达了一种邪恶的印象。

衙门通常分多个庭院,这些庭院都是供衙门小吏及官员家人居住的地方。一天的工作结束后,官员会在其中一个庭院内接待自己的朋友们,安然抽着烟,或者下中国象棋,这种象棋的规则复杂,我们的象棋是中国象棋的简化版。有时候,工作之后,官员也会沉迷于大烟枪带来的愉悦中,就像19世纪我们的好酒之徒喝酒一样。已故的两江总督刘坤一就是个吸食鸦片的人,他和署理两江总督张之洞协同努力,使长江沿岸各省份在义和团运动爆发期间依然一片祥和。不过有一件事他从未做过,那就是焦急。他认为,匆忙轻率是不体面的行为,他鄙视这种行为。处理公务时,他会使用在我们英国的宫廷中所不接受的理念,不过在中国,上至天子,下至平民,大家都理解并且认可这些理论。关于我们称为官场腐败的论理问题,可以写很多相关的内容,但还是让事情维持现状吧,人民和政府都能够理解，并且也没有人对这些贪腐进行公然的抗议和反对。我们也不能忘记，官场的"不规范"现象在世界各地都是普遍存在的。

中国官员的社交生活可不仅限于他自己的衙门之内。他很喜欢跟自己的朋友们相聚，一边高谈阔论，一边喝茶。在欧洲，我们想象不到中国主人准备的最好的茶叶是一道多么精美的佳肴。到中国人家里做客，主人会自己泡茶，茶叶只在新烧开的水里泡4—5分钟，然后就被倒入精致的瓷杯之中，这种杯子只有我们用的利口杯那么大，不加牛奶和糖，直接饮用。喝完茶之后，杯子里仍然能闻到茶的清香，很好闻。

第 六 章

富人的房屋都建在广州城的东部,并且都有高墙隔离街道。从前门进入富人家,客人要经过多座院落和会客厅。这些建筑由经过精雕细琢的花岗岩石柱支撑,为了将自己的家建设得奢华而不失格调,中国的富翁可谓是不惜一切代价。通过庭院可进入花园,花园里总会有一个池塘,池塘里栽种着睡莲、荷花等花卉,还养着一群金鱼。花园里通常还有一座假山,假山上还有洞

第六章

穴，配备着数条幽静的小道，池塘上还有一座小桥，桥有棱有角的，就像在那些古老的青瓷盘上看到的那样。桥曲曲折折通往塘中的小岛，岛上有一座精美的茶亭。在一栋无主大房子里，我见到一些做工精良的锻造铁制品样本，这些铁制品包括草、芦苇、花等形状，每件铁制品都放在两片玻璃夹着的橱窗里。这些铁制品样本的历史可追溯至约450年前，那名制作工匠至今仍然受到人们的尊重和敬仰。有人曾想出巨资收购这些铁制品，不过主人将这些东西视作比黄金更珍贵的宝物，不愿出售。

广州最大的特色之一就是花艇，大量的花艇聚集到一起，形成一条路。这些船上都是餐馆，纨绔子弟经常来这里举行宴会，享用饕餮大餐，还可尽情享乐。花艇老板会给每位客人提供4—5个年轻女孩，她们坐在男士们身后，为他们助兴。由于宴会要举行很长时间，有很多个环节，客人们无须参与宴会的整个过程，一位客人有时只参加其中的一两个环节。过程中还有人奏乐唱歌，可能还有别的我没有仔细留意的其他娱乐项目，不过，还是要说，中国有受到制约的风俗习惯，这是人们公开承认的，比侵蚀西方文明内核的弊病危害要小得多。

官员们的妻子和女儿们都住在条件差一点的小城镇

里，按照规矩，她们只能去拜访跟自己身份地位差不多的人，而这种人极少居住在小城之中。在大城市里，她们可以去拜访富商家的女眷，而且绝不缺乏可聊的话题。她们对公众事务很感兴趣，而且对热门话题施加了不小的影响力。中国的许多女士都很有教养，如果出现了与自己的福利息息相关的事，她们都会毫不犹豫地表达自己的看法。不久前，广州城里爆发了一次妇女集会，抗议一项不得人心的规定。在中国传教的欧洲人让中国各阶层的女士们都开始学习英语，现在许多女士都能说一口流利的英语。中国的改革家康有为，从北京飞抵香港来避难时，他的女儿还只会说她熟悉的中文，全家定居海峡殖民地[①]两年之后，她经香港去美国继续学习时，英语就说得很流利了。

影响整个中国的改革浪潮决不仅限男人参与。1900年，上海举行了一次女性联合会议，会议主席是英国的卜力夫人，主题是中国女性的家庭生活。会议举行了4天时间，其间中国和欧洲妇女都阅读了很多论文，这些论文是

---

① 海峡殖民地，英国在1826—1946年对位于马来半岛的3个重要港口和马来群岛各殖民地的管理建制。——译者注

第六章

关于影响中国各阶层女士的各种问题和社会习俗的。会议涵盖的议题很多,包含了一系列内容:孩子的抚养、婆媳问题、娃娃亲、中国的女仆制、裹足、婚葬和社交习俗等,会议过程中出现了许多关于这个泱泱大国的女性的生活状况和习俗的珍贵的一手描述。会议结束时,主席卜力夫人作了如下总结:

> 本次会议选择"中国女性的家庭生活"作为讨论的主题,现在我们要来作个总结。我相信,我们对这些论文和报告都很感兴趣,这些资料里有许多关于这个辽阔国家各个地区的内容,我们大部分人都从未听说过。我发现,大部分中国女性,尤其是社会等级较低的女性,她们的状况比我所想象的还要差。例如,女仆们的艰难命运,必定会激起那些对别人的苦难有恻隐之心的男男女女的同情。不过,虽然我们了解了中国女性生活的阴暗面,但我们不

能忘记,没有光就没有阴影,因此,许多中国女性生活中也有光明的一面,我们读到的一些论文显示,不少中国女性,虽然从未受过欧洲的影响,但却有高贵的品质,并且对那些急需帮助、境况不如自己的邻人乐善好施。也许我们中的一些人容易以评判下层的标准来评判中国的中上阶层,而欧洲人通常受到中国下层的粗鲁对待。我们住在古老教堂和庄园中的居民怎会忍受外国人用评判我们社会底层和流浪汉的标准来评判我们?在其他国家中,这些社会底层人士往往给自己的国家带来羞辱。由于习惯成自然,同样,我们习以为常的事就不那么可怕了,即使它本质上是不好的,我不禁希望,对我们来说炼狱般的事情对中国女性就不那么糟糕了。我只能希望那些即使在裹足这件事上仍因自尊心而说不感觉疼的人,她们遭受的痛苦能因习惯而有所缓解。

毫无疑问,裹足会给女性的身心健康造成严重的损害,如今我们发现,中国很多地方的女性中都燃起了反抗裹足的火花,这一点令人感到欣慰。由于新思想已经渗入了中国,我一点也不怀疑,中国的女性会跟其他国家的女性一样,不再做不合时宜的时

第六章

尚或礼俗的奴隶。我不禁想到，中国女性所面临的更多病痛和不适，一定得由中国人自己根除，我们这些外国人所能做的，便是在力所能及的范围内提供她们所需的途径。年复一年，中国接受教育和启蒙的女性会越来越多，她们都接受了西方科学和思维方式的训练，而且还都会保有自己原本的个性，因此她们每个人都像是一个光源，灿烂的光芒能够照耀到她们的同胞身上。曾经，有人送给我一朵花，这种花有一段非凡的历史。他告诉我，在希腊的某地，发现了一个据传是古希腊人开采过的矿藏处，地里布满了成堆的石头和垃圾。古希腊人的才华在某种程度上远胜现代人，虽然他们不懂如今的科技向我们揭示的道理，但检查这些扔在古老矿藏外的石块和垃圾时，人们发现多数石块和垃圾中富含矿石，这是前人都未曾发现过的，而且数量很多，值得变废为宝，提取这种潜在的财富，于是人们把石头搬走，去进行熔炼等加工，石头移开之后，地上便生出了许多植物，开出黄色的小花，这种花园丁以前都没有见过。据推测，这些花的种子被压在石头下已经有多个世纪了。中国不也是这样吗？她的怀抱里隐藏的进步的种子正在休眠，因为自上而下的旧思想压制而无法破土而出，而土壤里可能也有值得开发的矿石，为了保存这些矿石，必须把它们提炼出来；为了让真理、幸福和纯洁的花朵在这片土地上竞相开放，这些重重的石头必须被移开。压在这些花朵种子之上的最重的两堆"垃圾"名叫"愚昧"和"偏见"。我深信，我们在此次会议上所收集到的资料能够帮你们移走这两堆"垃圾"。

按照东方习俗，无论是选择自己的妻子，还是通过家庭关系结交女士都应该谨慎，中国的女士们无疑都是温情脉脉的妻子和母亲。笔者知道，澳门的一位寡妇，她的渔民丈夫因出海捕鱼失事丧命之后，她每天都在海边徘徊，挥舞着丈夫生前穿的外套，在那里焚香祷告，不停地召唤，希望丈夫能够回到她身边，这场面真令人痛心；笔者

第六章

也见过在一条流淌的小溪旁,那些心神不宁的女人把生病的孩子的衣服放到熊熊燃烧的火上来回挥舞,呼唤她们所敬拜的神为生病的孩子去病消灾、驱赶邪魔。确实,按照中国人的普遍观念,对一个家庭而言,失去丈夫的痛苦比不上失去唯一的儿子的痛苦,因为家族的荣誉一般都是由男性继承人去捍卫的,而缺少继承人,家族的世系也就没有合适的形式来传承。中国人显然对迷信观念表示恐惧,但还有拯救信仰的办法,中国人尤其希望逝者在来世过得舒适,会考虑逝者的需求。在香港时,笔者曾见过两个女人很郑重地搬着用薄纸和轻便的竹子制作的小屋、桌子、椅子和马的模型,去一个空旷的地方恭敬地焚烧掉,无疑是为了离世的丈夫而焚烧的。斯堪的纳维亚人也相信来世,人下葬的时候,生前用的船、战马和武器也会埋在他们身旁。

孩子降生时,家里的长辈们会用薄纸做一只小船,绑在一小捆稻草上,然后将船放进河水里,如果小船顺流漂走了,那就意味着孩子的一生顺利无忧,如果被水冲到了岸上,那么全家人都会非常担忧，因为这意味着命运之神不看好这孩子。如果家庭成员在海上丧生，家人们同样会放小船到海中，船里还放着小人，小人脚下堆着金纸银纸，以代替钱。在香港港口，我们总是能见到这样的船在海水中漂荡，每一只都象征着深切的悲痛，表现了全人类潜意识中对冥界的亲人的绝望的焦虑。

这就是中国人生活的悲伤一面，尤其是那些穷苦人家。而中国的女性，虽然享乐的方式跟西方不同，但社交方面需要讲究的礼仪一点也不比西方的女性少。她们不喜欢剧烈的体育运动——所有的东方人都将我们引人注目的男子气概视作未解之谜——不过她们间一直没有停止过相互拜访，拜访之前就要做以下准备工作——涂脂抹粉、做发型、精心挑选合适的华美服装，就像太阳王路易十四后宫中的美女化妆一样有趣。对欧洲男人而言，中国女性的衣着似乎是不变的——一件刺绣精美的宽松短上衣，一条百褶长裙和宽大的裤子，呈深红色、黄色或五彩缤纷——这些可能西方的女士更熟悉吧。无疑中国的丈夫和父亲们也知道，家里的女性是爱美的，所以他们对家中的女性都很慷慨大方。基本的衣服式样是不变的，因为在中国，女士展示自己的身材是不雅的，但中国的服装制造商总是不

第六章

停地变换衣服上的刺绣式样,就像那些法国同行们改变礼服的式样一样。因此,大城市里总有漂亮的刺绣服装因跟不上无情的潮流而被丢弃,就像西方那些追逐时髦的女性所做的一样。

在中国,拜访别人之前需要做的准备工作也是很讲究的,就跟所有其他的社交礼仪一样;深红色的名帖,3—4英寸宽,而有时长度可达1英尺——名帖的尺寸大小跟拜访者的社会地位相关——到主人家后,先送上名帖,然后主人会派仆人送一封邀请函给客人,让客人进门,女主人穿上最好的服装,在大门、第二道门或第三道门前迎接客人,位置由来宾的社会地位决定,客人进入房间时有一套复杂的仪式。客人进门之后,女人们谈论的都是女人们的话题,这些似乎是全世界女人都感兴趣的话题。大家交谈的话题包括鸦片,可能还有书籍、孩子、家里的厨子、社

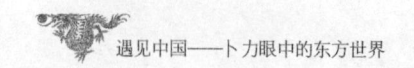

会事件以及当地的政局等,形成了舆论的导向。中国的社会风俗不容许传播谣言,不过谁会保证不传播呢?连中国的爱神都既足智多谋,又爱恶作剧。中国人也会沉迷游戏,他们玩的牌就跟他们的象棋一样,规则复杂难懂。

如果客人还带了小孩,小孩子也都会得到礼物,他们从来没有忽略过这种细致的关心。确实,按照既定的中国习俗,在中国新年和其他节日里,人们会互赠礼物。

第 七 章

1841年,英国人初到香港时,香港不过是一个人烟稀少的荒岛,而如今,香港有居民377 000人,其中有36万中国人。维多利亚城位于香港港口南岸,是仅次于伦敦的世界第二大货运港口,城市背靠高度超过1800英尺的陡峭山坡,原本崎岖的山崖上,修建了稳固的公路,点缀着宏伟的建筑,还有一条架空索道通往海拔1200英尺的峰顶,这里海拔相对较高,气温比海平面要低,所以夏天的时候,欧洲居民可以来这里躲避山下难耐的高温。很难说香港从维多利亚港看更漂亮还是从山顶看更漂亮。从港湾看,拥挤的城市被宽广的海岸包围着的,沿着山势往上,从街道到梯田,再到别墅,一直到山顶——梯田和别墅被裹在常青的热带植物群中,有树木、灌木和攀缘类植物等,峰顶还有浅蓝色的绣球花，海拔低点的地方有紫色的簕杜鹃、黄色的黄蝉等，全部沉浸在阳光之中，争奇斗艳，这种景象在温带很难见到。而头顶上，湛蓝的天空中轻轻飘浮着洁白的云朵。

远远向东望去是跑马地①，呈扁平的椭圆形，四周的山坡上有一片片公共墓地，堪称是世界上最精致美观的墓地。无论是基督教徒还是伊斯兰教徒，无论是东方人还是西方人，都从劳碌中解脱出来，安眠于此。而在墓地下方的椭圆形山谷中，各种英国式的体育运动和比赛正如火如荼地进行着。

从太平山顶俯瞰香港这座城市和海港，我们能看到九龙这座平坦的半岛，还有从东面一直蔓延到西面的崎岖的山群。不过，香港最吸引人的地方是海港，豪华大气，蔚蓝色的怀抱里倚靠着与远东地区进行商贸活动的各国的大汽船，周围还有350艘汽艇，海港以此为傲，它们在拥挤的海港中全速行驶，证明了中国船员惊人的胆略。在海港外，往昂船洲的方向，能看到美式的纵帆船高高的桅杆，

---

① 跑马地，香港最早的赛马场在此兴建，如今仍举行赛马活动，并成为高级住宅区。——译者注

有的船长——可能也是船主——也会携妻子到船上，船尾有住宿舱，这样的配置连我们英国最大班轮的船长见了也会眼红，还有数千艘各种各样的中国船只像成群的苍蝇一样聚集在海湾滔天的海水中。这里听不到城市的喧嚣，即便是那些汽船吊杆升降和卸货时刺耳的声音在这里也显得轻柔，诉说着它们商业活动的故事。

晚上，这里的景色更加迷人，因为海上和岸边有无数的灯光闪烁跳跃。海岸线在灯光的映衬下显得格外醒目，黑漆漆的海面上倒映出来的星光似乎比别处更加耀眼，与船上的万点灯光交相辉映。

天气暖和的时候，香港通常就是上文所述的那样，但是到冬天，香港还是很冷，需要借助火和毛皮来取暖。不过美丽的海港遭遇可怕的台风侵袭时则是另一番景象。不熟悉香港的人，台风来之前是看不出不正常的，他们如果看到20多艘舢板和驳船，被汽艇拖到避难所——铜锣湾，一定还会很惊讶；不过东南方天际滚滚的乌云、猛烈的风、骤降的气压以及"龙吸水"的景观，这些迹象都在提醒细心的气象预报员，要给人们发出警告了，此外，海上东南方向的海浪也提醒谨慎的船长，除非两个锚都抛下去了，并且燃料充足，否则不要进入狭窄的水域。

天阴沉沉的，风势越来越猛，海上的风暴在所难免，岸边以及海上的人们都在忙着为躲避和应对积极做准备。缆绳加长了，桅杆顶端的东西都收拾好了，海上升起了蒸汽。岸上所有的窗户都用对抗台风的栅栏锁好了，因为如果来势汹汹的台风将窗子刮走了，那么它所造成的损害就无法预估了。有时候，房屋的墙壁都会被风拔起，而屋内的东西被刮走摔碎在山坡上。曾有一天清晨，我就亲眼见证过九龙的台风风势增到最大时的情形。整个港口厚厚的水沫四溅，水沫后面的浪头如魔鬼般疯狂地翻涌，我们看到，浪花在九龙港高高的码头上不断涌上来，又退下去，淹没了先前的码头和仓库，在呼啸的风声中，失事船只透过海水和薄雾发射炮弹求救，在强劲的台风的呼号中，听起来却像沉闷的轰响，他们在不断呼救，却没有人能够施救。上午10点，台风继续北上，留下了海港里一片狼藉，很多大船和舢板船在港口沉没，九龙码头的小船碎片铺了一英里多长，大海逐渐恢复了平静，数百名受害者葬身海底，港口的海面上漂浮着无数的货物包。

台风这类事故倒是充分体现了中国人的组织能力。等到海面足够平静，能够通行汽艇的时候，我派人去请一位中国绅士，并向他提议，我们应该去救助那些难民，援救需要帮助的人，但是我迟了一步，同业公会已经派遣了两艘强力汽艇，一艘放着棺材，准备给溺亡者，另一艘上有一名医生，携带了必要的救援物品去救助伤者，还有一些食物，去送给那些在灾害中失去了所有家当的人们。我乘船沿着九龙港的海岸前行了一个小时，遭台风侵袭的船只残骸在海堤旁堆了二三十英尺宽，跟我所想象的不一样，这里没有人露出茫然和失望的神情，所有的船民，无论男女老幼，存活下来的人们都像蜜蜂一样辛勤劳作着，所有人都希望能从家园的废墟中抢救回一点什么，男人们从漂浮着残骸一处跳到另一处，有时潜到水里，他们与残酷的命运作着斗争，但他们仍默默接受这不可避免的命运。

虽然当时的香港受殖民统治，但它本质上仍然是一个中式的城市。这里的街道受英国管理的影响建得宽阔，房屋精致而牢固，只保留了少部分卫生局创立前的房屋，通过细致而坚持不懈的检查，房屋和周围环境的干净整洁得到保证。店铺融合了欧式建筑风格和中式的装修风格，造型精雕细琢，色彩明艳光鲜。外部还配有挂饰，给香港的街头增添了艳丽的色彩。除了大港口的码头汗流浃背的苦力，中国人普遍喜欢穿蓝色的衣服，忙碌的街头熙熙攘攘都是身着蓝色衣物的人，跟街头绚丽的色彩融合在一起。我们称为大街的主干道上有银行、酒店和欧洲主要公司的账房，以及更适合欧洲居民和旅客的店铺，这些宏伟的建筑跟欧洲城市建筑的风格差不多，店铺里有各种买家所需的欧洲商品，还有吸引游客的中国和日本货物。不过这座城市最富裕的区域还是中国人的居住区，这里的房产交易价格很高，有的地方一英亩（按现在的换算制，一英亩约合4047平方米）地16万英镑。这里的店铺都是中国人所有，店铺经营各行各业，医生挂起了招牌，声称自己治好了骨折的腿，牙医则放了一块木板，上面悬挂着5—6排尺寸惊人的白齿模型，演示了龋齿的各个阶段。充满无尽动力的人随处可见。黄包车匆匆驶过，这种方便出行的出租黄包车只有一名苦力来拉，而私家的黄包车除了拉车者，后面还有一两位仆人在推；更稳当的轿辇经过，有

2—4个苦力担抬，前后方的轿夫每次都用不同的脚抬步，这样能防止轿辇摇晃。这里的商铺都没有玻璃门，而且一直都是开着的，到了夜晚，商铺停止营业，门都用厚木板封上，最后的两块木板用一根门闩固定住。这样，外面的人就无法破门而入；但也有些案件里，手持武器的盗贼在关门的最后一刻偷偷溜进来，藏在门板里，确保自己不被人发现，然后掏出武器，盗走抽屉里的钱物，将恐慌的房主和仆人绑起来、塞住嘴，然后逃之夭夭。

香港的早晨很有意思。早晨5点，人们就起床了。工人们都在街边的店铺吃早餐，桌子都摆在街边，上面摆满了米饭和粥（米饭和水的混合物），还有已经摘择好了的各种蔬菜、肉类，包括生的家禽内脏、鱼片，以及酱油和其他调味品。

饥肠辘辘的食客会得到半碗米饭,再放上各类蔬菜和一片肉或者一些切碎的家禽内脏,再在菜上面浇上一勺滚烫的粥,早餐就做好了。食客将碗送到嘴边,用筷子拨一大口饭送到张开的嘴里,然后从碗里拣出美味的菜肴,把菜肴送到还未经咀嚼的米饭上,然后闭上嘴巴,咀嚼、吞咽。每一口都要品味很久,这个过程一直重复到早餐吃完为止。桌子附近可能还有售卖海螺的,这可是大众青睐的一种食物,尤其是男孩们,他们把所有运气都押在填饱肚子上。这些海螺都放在篮子里,篮子的把手处放着几条金属丝,这些金属丝都被系在长长的绳索上。一个小男孩来买海螺,将钱放在货摊上,同时从一根装满了竹片的长竹节里取出一块。有的竹片末端有一个数字,有的则是空白,这些爱碰运气的人可能发现自己第一次抽到的是空白竹片,但他也可能足够幸运一下就抽中了带数字的竹片,数字代表他即将吃到的海螺个数,然后他很熟练地用那些弯弯绕绕的金属丝将螺肉挑出来吃掉。男孩们都活泼又调皮,而弯曲的金属丝很耗钱，所以，孩子们要"就地"吃完，谨慎的摊主决不允许金属丝与绳索脱离。用猪油煎炸的糯米饭团也是一种广受欢迎的街头小吃，华人社区里经常能见到黏性惊人的甜食和可疑的食材。早晨的人们总是心情愉悦的，他们发自内心地开玩笑、大笑，这种情景完全与欧洲人对中国人的印象不相符，我们总认为中国人是思想麻木、缺乏情感表达的。

中国人一天只吃两餐。早餐时间为6—8点之间，午餐时间为下午4点。

此时，从九龙来的船送来了蔬菜，小贩们忙着将这些菜卖给千家万户，城外的菜农每天都要打理自家的菜园，种菜很有一套，因此菜的长势也非常好。没有比药店生意更好的了，中国人总认为用"天然"的才是最好的，如将虎牙、蛇脊焙烧，制成一种直径为3/4英寸的神秘药丸，我们不知道这种药丸的疗效，可能只会有精神效用吧。中国农历新年的这一天，每家每户门前都要挂一小把植物，包括5种植物：菖蒲，代表了刀剑；大戟，代表一种铁制的战斗兵器，用以抵御恶魔；洋葱，可以抵抗疟疾之神；艾草和乌韭。这种符咒跟石莲花一样灵验，在想象中国家形成前的时代，爱尔兰的农舍屋顶上都会精心种植这种植物，

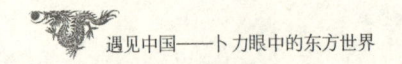

以保护自己不受火灾侵扰。

不过，早晨最忙碌的人应该是理发师，因为中国的劳工自己不剃头，所以每天早晨，每家理发店里都聚集了一小群人在等待理发，大家都在热火朝天地聊天，还有人一边等一边读晨报。无论有多少人在等待，理发师总是不急不躁地忙碌着，不仅给客人剃前面的头发，还会修剪眉毛和睫毛，然后就是仔细地清理客人的耳朵，这些做完后，理发师给客人用洗发液洗头，并给他按摩，最后，客人又坐在椅子上，身体前倾，理发师用力捶打客人的后脑勺和侧面，手法一点也不轻柔，当理发师的空掌在客人头上响亮地拍了一下时，表示理发结束。大家普遍认为总是对耳朵的清洗是有害的，这可能会导致耳聋，不过如果不清洗这里，客人便认为这次理发不值30钱——修剪头发通常是这个价格，约合1分钱的1/3。最后，理发师还要帮客人把辫子编好，真的头发和假的头发混搭，辫子很长，几乎拖到脚后跟，再将头发的末端用一根丝绸流苏束好。有的男人也会自己编辫子，只要将头发铺在木梯的横木上，然后双手向后编辫子，一边编一边将头发拉紧。

对普通游客来说，木匠和石匠是最常见的两种技工，

第七章

直径两英尺的方木，木匠一下就锯开了，令观者感到惊讶。将木头放好之后，木匠踩在木头上，只用一把框锯，就能把木头锯好。这种工作看起来十分费力，而木匠每天要锯很多木头。而石匠的工作就轻松多了。中国人很擅长凿石，用铁或木楔裁好大块的花岗岩石料，用铁制的凿子在石料上凿孔，如果要凿很深很宽的孔，那么先凿好一个小孔，然后将木楔推进去，用水把木楔浸湿，使其膨胀，推动石料出来，再将石料稍作修整，整个过程就是这样。

东西方人的身体形态唯一的不同就是东方人能够坐在自己的脚后跟上。亚洲人坐在自己的后跟上，也能跟欧洲人坐在椅子上一样悠闲自在；凿石的时候，工人会跪坐在自己凿刻的石头上，沿石头边缘垂直向下凿刻。工匠们按这种姿势坐成一排，从远处看去，就像是停靠在悬崖峭壁上的一群秃鹫。

在香港，最低等的体力工作就是苦力，他们将煤和建筑材料运送到山顶；从中我们看到了计件工作劳动者的坚忍勤勉与非凡创造力，这确保了他们从每日的劳动中获得最大的收获。在陡峭的山上，建造房舍用的每一块砖和每一篮沙土都是苦力肩挑来的，每次都用一根竹扁担挑两篮，薪酬按挑担的重量计算。每一担可重达一英担[1]，人负载这个重量，走过两英里左右十分陡峭的道路，速度缓慢，中途时常要停下来，苦力尽量将休息的时间减到最少。有时一个人同时带两担，把其中一担送到50码以外的地方，然后放下来，回去挑第二担，这一担要挑到距原出发点100码远的地方，放下第二担，他或她还得返回将第一担再次挑到距第二担50码远的前方。在山里挑担的不仅仅有男人，也还有年老体弱的女人，他们都得这样反复地运送，直到到达目的地为止。途中没有任何停靠站，也没有休息的地方，唯一的休息就是放下一担返回去挑另一担的这段路。因为要将货物运送到山顶，没有人能够不停下来休息，一次性挑上山，所以这种运送方式节省了休息的时间。

  一天的工作结束之后，劳动者并不爱去酒馆。他们非常喜欢游戏，更严格地来说应该是赌博；虽然有打压赌场的严格限令，但官方的明文禁令都无法绝对禁止人们去摇骰玩牌。人们用的赌博工具不仅限于牌和骰子，用瓜子或其他自然界产物都可以下注，用这些东西赌博，

---

[1] 英担，英制重量单位，1英担约等于50.802千克。——译者注

如果警察中有爱管闲事的人来检查，也找不到任何证据。"猜枚"这种游戏不仅劳工们爱玩，社会各阶层人士都喜欢，游戏的过程中，人们发出的喊叫声和笑声让附近的邻居无法安眠、抱怨连连。游戏的规则很简单，是双人玩的游戏。一个人突然伸出一根、两根或更多的手指，另一个人在对方伸出手时喊出手指的个数。英国的冰上溜石（掷冰壶）游戏也是一个喧闹的游戏，不过，游戏者发出的喧闹声音总比不过两个激动的玩猜枚的人。人们可能认为，猜手指的数量是一个只能靠运气的游戏，不过，一位中国绅士曾告诉我，伸出的是一根、两根、三根还是更多根手指，手部的肌肉有一点点差别，而这种差别非常微弱，只有专业的玩家才能辨识出来。

比起中国的成人喜欢坐着玩游戏，学童还是喜欢爱跑爱跳、很有活力的游戏。他们迅速地熟悉了欧洲的游戏，如板球和足球等，不过他们也总会玩"跳房

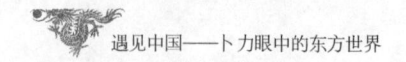

子"游戏，这种游戏跟英国村庄里盛行的那种差不多。如果能围成一圈，他们还会踢毽子玩，只需要一个软木塞和两三根鸟类的羽毛便能制作出一个毽子，羽毛是用来控制木塞的起落的。这种游戏只需用脚，孩子们非常灵敏地相互踢来踢去。毽子通常能 5—10 分钟不落地，人的眼和手配合要高度默契才可以做到。

第八章

有一种运动，中国成年人表现得非常出色，那就是赛龙舟。每年6月，端午节期间，船夫和渔民总要赛龙舟。龙舟约90英尺长，中间有横梁，宽度仅够两名桨手并排而坐。龙舟里要坐60—80名桨手，龙舟中间还站着一位，他面前有一面鼓或锣，桨手们划船时，他要按节奏敲打锣鼓，桨手们的划桨速度与这个节奏要保持一致。一人站在船尾，手中握着一根长长的划桨，一个男孩坐在龙舟前面，手里握着两根被绑在船首龙头上的绳索，它们把龙头装饰得熠熠生辉，绳索不断地被拉动，龙头也随之左右转动。两艘参与竞赛的船划到了出发的浮标前，裁判一个手势示意，比赛就开始了。掌控节奏的人疯狂地敲锣打鼓，鼓舞桨手们，船上近200把桨激烈而有节奏地划动着，水花四溅，色彩鲜艳的龙头不断地转动，真是壮观而振奋人心的场面。桨手们的肌肉紧绷，这世上再没有哪种运动比这更需要肌肉力量了。有时候，竞争激烈，船会发生碰撞，这种情况下必须重赛，因为船桨交叠在一起，如果不停下来是没法解决的。但是这样的意外事故不会引起不快和纠纷，大家都会心平气和地对待，这只不过意味着重赛一次而已。广州城内的珠江河段上，很多船只停靠在河边来看比赛。比赛时没有警察或负责人监管，不过没有船只会破坏纪律或给比赛造成阻碍。

中国人向往过节，喜欢大场面，这充分显示了他们的组织能力。澳门最盛大的节日是为了纪念李天王之子哪吒的，每隔10年的闰月就要为此举行游行庆典[①]。这是各行

[①] 实际上，澳门每年农历五月十八日都会庆祝哪吒诞辰，此处作者所知信息有误。——译者注

第八章

各业人的集会——钟表匠、裁缝、鞋匠,等等。每个行会的游行队伍的前面都会有一个人扛着一面绣工精巧的巨大三角形旗帜,还会有人打着一把大伞,象征着这个行业的荣耀。许多人手里拿的竹竿上有刺绣的横幅。还有人抬着几把平常大小的装饰精美的椅子,有的上面放着敬献给神明的供品,有的则放着木鼓。每个行会都有自己的乐队:一些中式弦类乐器、簧管乐器和锣、琵琶等,琵琶这种乐器通常是举过头顶或是安放在脖子后面演奏的①。各行会成员都两两并排跟在乐队后行进,成员们都穿着淡紫色的丝质衣服,腰上系着一条红色或黄色的宽腰带,腰带两头绣着精致的图案,一直拖到腿边。钟表匠行会成员们的右胸上都挂着表。游行队伍中还有孩子们穿着华丽的中古服装,骑在经过精心装扮的小马上。有的行会则用车载着孩子游行,孩子们在车上做着各种动作,有时还能看到一个孩子将剑刺穿另一个孩子胸部和背部,这并不是真正的刺杀,只是在孩子身上巧妙地安装了一个铁框架。行会游行的团体多种多样,整个队伍不时停下来时,孩子们就可以

① 此处所描述的琵琶演奏姿势与常识不符,推测作者可能受四大天王佛像中艺术化处理的影响。——译者注

下来休息，那些铁架子也从身上取下来。与此同时，行会队伍里持伞的成人，会让孩子们聚集到伞下来，以避免太阳暴晒。

每个行会都带着苦力，搬运凳子，队伍一停止行进，队员就马上坐下来；而锣声敲响，示意大家继续前行的时候，苦力就搬起凳子，跟随队伍继续前进。

队伍的最后是一条长龙，由26个人抬。龙身长140英尺，背上是绿色和银色的龙鳞，周身披着红色、绿色、粉色和黄色的丝绸缎带。龙前面有一个人，带着一个大球在龙前舞动，这个球就代表月亮。龙追着月亮不断地从街的一端冲向另一端，却被另一人阻碍，那人手中持有一个旁边镶有金线的球，或许这个球代表着太阳，正在拯救月亮，不让它被龙吞噬，人们认为发生月食就是因为龙吞噬了月亮。龙不断在街边蜿蜒徘徊，只要有足够的空间，它就会不断翻腾，不过一旦尾巴碰到了镶嵌着金线的球，它就马上舒展开来。要通过指定的地点，整支队伍要耗时一个半小时，但观众的秩序井然，始终都有足够的场地供舞龙者表演。最终，每一行业的游行队伍，都到达了自己的目的地，那些游行时的装饰物都被精心收藏起来，以待将来再用。

这样的节日当然只是澳门当地的节日，而中国唯一的法定假日就是农历新年，这一天，所有的行业都暂停营业。总督会放下自己的印章；地方官们也是如此；商人们关上店铺，收好他的账本，而他们的伙计们则趁机回乡下的老家探亲。店主会给伙计们举办一场宴会，结束的时候，店主还要演讲一番，祝福大家"新年快乐"，在某些情况下还会说："我希望，你，还有你（提到其中一些伙计的名字），来年会找到更好的工作。"这话就是微妙的暗示，以上提到了名字的人将会被解雇。在中国，通常所有生意上的事在新年这天都会暂停并结清，所有的债务也应在新年之前偿还清楚。

在香港，新年时所有商业活动都要暂停10天，这时候，华人区的很多街道两侧都会建起货摊，货摊上有各种吸引人的玩意儿，因此街道上总是人声鼎沸。市面上还有一种白色钟形花十分畅销，就像很大的欧石楠一样，这种花被称为"年花"；街上摆着许多装着金鱼的球形玻璃鱼缸，过新年时，人们都赶着来买。因过年而临时搭起的货摊下，有各阶层都喜欢的物件。各种库存的商品，流动摊贩和店铺都摆出来了，他们希望在这段时间里赚一笔。所有的东西都可能从这里买到，从铜器、瓷器再到泥塑，价廉物美。有时候，收藏者可以经过二手交易买到真正有价值的东西；而满心渴望的小孩子们在这里会买些便宜的小物件。这种年度集市很好地证明了中国人的一种特质，所有出售的物件和画作，都没有任何不合礼节的迹象。

过新年时，每家门上都插着一个由孔雀羽毛制成的小装饰物，这象征着吉祥如意。大家庆祝的方式丰富多彩，而且非常热闹。正月里，大家都带着礼物，去别人家拜年；还去上坟，祭祀先人。新年期间，大家都燃放鞭炮和烟花庆祝，一长串花费不低的鞭炮从楼上的阳台上挂下来，点燃之后鞭炮声震耳欲聋，持续好几分钟，整条街道上都能听到，像步枪和火炮发出的声音。节后，街道上满是包裹鞭炮的红纸碎屑。

在香港，除了新年集市，最吸引人的活动就是一年一度的赛马会。观看比赛的，除了香港人，还有广州和广东其他偏远地方的人们。赛马这种活动，起源于欧洲，却在中国的各港口城市中逐渐盛行，这些马都是来自蒙古的小型马，身强体壮。赛事盛大壮观，赛期一共 3 天，按习俗，其间可以尽情狂欢，警方对违反赌博法规的行为睁一只眼闭一只眼，但会重拳打击暗藏机关的博彩盒、灌铅的骰子和其他不公平的赌博手段。赌徒们在赛事的间隙设局赌马，赛马会期间，他们能一睹这变化多端的奇妙的比赛风采，这种比赛既注重骑手的技能，也还要看机遇。

在香港，还有一种赌博游戏，我在别的地方从未见过。在一块平整的石头四周画一个圆圈，直径约 5 英尺，从圆心到圆周，划分出不同的区间，庄家在石头上放一堆铜币，赌博者把赌注下到选中的区域，然后庄家拿一个重物放在头上，他头猛得一甩将石头抛到 12 英尺远的地方，如果这个重物砸到了他自己放铜币的区间，那么他就赢得了圆圈中的所有赌注，而如果重物落到了其他放钱的区间，那么把注下在那个区域的玩家就赢得了石头上庄家放的那一堆钱币。

还有一种赌博，一块木板上面画着几幅人像，玩家们选择一个人物下注。随后庄家给玩家一个装有许多圆片的袋子，这些圆片有点像国际跳棋棋子，每一个圆片上面都有一个人物，庄家从袋子里取出一把圆片放在桌子上，分类，将与木板上画像一致的圆片放到各幅画像上，有多少圆片与木板上的一幅画像一致，那在这幅画像上下注的玩家就可以赢得多少倍的赌注，而如果取出的圆片上的画像，都与木板上的画像不符，那就输了。

为了杜绝瘟疫的肆虐，人们摒弃了对确实反常的现象视而不见的风俗，从而阻断成千上万"参赛"的寄生虫急速涌入香港，一旦破除了这种陋习，就不能让它再次恢复。

你不能认为，你走马观花地看遍了香港的街道，逛遍了户外好玩的地方，就玩遍了香港。香港还以有很多不错的学校而著称，皇仁学院和圣约翰学校就是其中两所规模最大的。还有一所极好的寄宿制学校，是为中国达官贵人的子女们开办的，这里的老师无微不至地监管学生；还有一所医学院，这里可以进行综合性的医疗教学；如今，这里还计划兴建一所综合性大学,将来可能成为中国学生接受高等教育的中心。

中国还没有完全意识到慈善机构的作用,不过,香港虽然不像欧洲那样有一般意义上的慈善机构,但私人慈善事业倒是很普及。穷人冬天能够得到私人捐赠的衣服,在饥荒爆发或是缺少粮食的情况下,有人会免费发放大米,或以低于成本的价格出售。如果有穷人饿死了,那么有人会提供棺材。在香港,中国人居住的社区里有一家装备精良的医院,对普通大众开放,还有一家鼠疫医院,过去的15年来,香港每年都要遭鼠疫侵袭,这家医院就是为感染了鼠疫的病人而开设的。

香港还有一所保良局,是东华医院的附属机构,这里收留孤儿,还有警方从人贩子手中解救的儿童,人贩子将这些孩子带进香港,把他们卖掉做家奴。保良局中的孩子们逐渐长大,男孩们到了能做事的年纪就会出去干活谋生,而女孩一到适婚年龄就会给她安排人家嫁出去。中国人常从这种机构中挑选女孩做妻子,这里也是失足或无依无靠的女孩的济良所,这样的

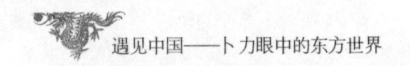

女孩后来也大多能找到丈夫，成立家庭。

我们这些外国人没有机会花长年的时间去观察中国社会生活，并探究其起源以及对社会产生的影响，上文所述只是中国生活片段的梗概。我们对中国的真实面貌所知甚少，一个普通欧洲人想到中国，就会将其定义为一个靠鸡鸣狗盗的手段兴起的国度，认为这里的国民狂傲自大，满嘴谎言，罪孽深重。另一方面，中国已经将与之打交道的西方强国当作恶霸，这些强国以毁灭性的力量来对付这个泱泱大国，并且强迫中国的皇帝及其政府，承认他们在中国的通商口岸拥有特许权。到目前为止，还没有听到中国人对这一点有所抱怨，但这并不意味着，那些受过教育的中国人对此都是麻木不仁的。日本在与中国的战争中取得的显著胜利，以及日本接受西方国家的文化科技迅速与外国平起平坐，这些引发了中国人的反思。我们不知道，什么时候重新考虑与世界各国的关系才会成为中国的当务之急。

慈禧皇太后和年轻的皇帝突然神秘离世，真是令人深感悲痛，新即位的皇帝还是个小孩，其父亲（摄政王）是一位思想先进开明的王公贵族。尽管中国的局势已经发生了巨大的改变，但更大的变化仍蓄势待发。多个世纪来的

第八章

闭关锁国政策已经有所松动，中国的近 3000 所学校都在教授英文，引入西方的教学理念。中国人开始考虑内部变革，已经确定要让所有的年轻人接受军事训练。如果中国抽出十分之一的人接受军事训练，那么就会形成一支 4000 万人的军队！这样的训练是否能培养出中国人的军事能力，不同的教育体系能不能引发中国的统治体制的剧烈变革，这还有待验证。在南方诸省，曾经赴美留学的学生形成了一股强劲的势力，他们多拥护共和制路线，不过笔者却发现，这一解决方案北方诸省的人们并不欢迎。

中国政府正在考虑设立市政委员会，这显然削弱了省级官员的专制权力。这种安排会不会增加政府职能部门的办事效率、减少贪污腐败，只能由时间来验证。但我们能够确定，无论改革者要求制度和风俗改革的呼声有多高，现在这一代人行动的速度都会很缓慢。中国人只有真正行动起来，中国才有可能取得稳定而持久的进步。只要中国人的军事潜能被激发出来了，到那时，外国人再也不能享

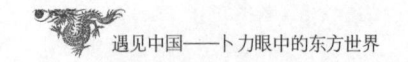

受对他们来说如此便利的治外法权了。

然而，如今，中国市场为世界制造业国家的激烈竞争提供了条件，在这种竞争中，英国极有可能被我们的德国同行击败，他们在商界的口号是"周密"，在其他领域里德国也是一样。

中国的觉醒意味着她要加入世界商贸战场的激烈竞争来争取她应得的全部份额。她的商业潜能巨大，生产能力也不容小觑，将来一定能够自给自足，并且也一定可以把自己的商品送入遥远的国外市场。根据笔者对中国的探查，过去的数年里，中国的影响力已遍及世界各地。在纽芬兰现已绝迹的比沃苏克人饰品中，在秘鲁印加文明遗迹被埋藏的陶器里，还有爱尔兰，发现了多个不同时期的中国陶瓷印章，有些埋得很深，从这些瓷器上篆刻的文字上来判断，这些东西的历史可追溯至公元 9 世纪。随着商贸活动的繁盛，工资上涨，中国的生产成本可能会提高到与其他国家相当的水平，如果不能达到这个水平，那将来的竞争，可能利物浦、伯明翰和曼彻斯特的工人，会为英国通过哄骗、折磨、欺凌、打击将这个远东巨人逼上商业道路而深感后悔，他们没想到中国的商业竟会发展得那么成功。中国有便宜的劳动力和无尽的矿藏，只要中国人掌握了操纵

第八章

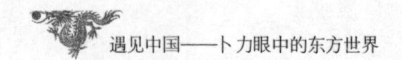

机械的技能，接受了教育开化的人能果敢地利用这些资源，那么中国就能成为强有力的竞争者，到时候几乎最强大的对手也会感到畏惧。

中国唯一不去跟别国竞争的是谁最懒散，所有国民都竭尽所能地为这个国家尽力，那么这个国度就会爆发出强劲的气势。

中国教育体系的改革，也将会让中国摆脱科举制度的束缚，学生不再只靠死记硬背去竞争，而代之以理性的思考，这样，中国就能成为在世界上影响举足轻重的强国。那时，我们希望，中英两国的关系能建立在互信和友好的基础上。

CHINA

By Sir Henry Arthur Blake
Illustrated by Mortimer Menpes

CONTENTS

CHAPTER I 135

Description of China—Her Early History—Tartar Garrisons—Chinese Soldiers—Family Life—Power of Parents—Foot-Binding

CHAPTER II 146

Marriage Customs—Ancestral Halls—Official Hierarchy—Competitive Examinations—Taxation—Punishments—Torture—Story of Circumstantial Evidence

CHAPTER III 161

Gradations of Chinese Society—Agriculture—*Fung Sui*—Pawn Offices—River Boats and Junks—The Bore at Haining—Fishing Industry—Piracy on Rivers—Li Hung Chang—The West River—Temples of the Seven Star Hills—Howlick

CHAPTER IV 179

The Yangtze—Opium—Conclusions of Singapore Commission—British and German Trade in the Far East—Town and Country Life—Chinese Cities—Peking—Temple of Agriculture—Spring Ceremony of Ploughing by the Emperor and his Court

CHAPTER V 192

Peasant Cultivators—Religious Beliefs—Theatricals—Famine—Life in Coast Cities—Canton—Guild-Houses—Beggar Guild—Official Reception by Viceroy—Chinese Writing—Life of an Official

CHAPTER VI 214

Houses of Wealthy Inhabitants—Flower-Boats—Reform Movement among Chinese Women—Shanghai Women's Convention—Women's Superstitions—Chinese Ladies—Fashions—Visiting

CHAPTER VII 223

General Description of Hong Kong—Happy Valley—Peak District—Night View of Harbour—Typhoon—Energy of Survivors—The Streets—Early Morning Life of the City—Chinese Workmen—The Barber—The Sawyer—The Stonecutter—The Coolie—Gambling—Some Street Games

CHAPTER VIII 235

Dragon-Boat Races—Festival at Macao—New Year—New Year Customs—Hong Kong Races—Curious Forms of Gambling—Charitable Institutions of Hong Kong—The Future of China

CHAPTER I

In attempting even a slight sketch of China, its physical features, or some of the manners and customs of the various peoples whom we designate broadly as the Chinese, the writer is confronted with the difficulty of its immensity. The continuous territory in Asia over which China rules or exercises a suzerainty is over 4,200,000 square miles, covering an area of 1,530,000 square miles, with a population of about 410,000,000, or about twelve and a half times the area of the United Kingdom, and ten times its population.

This area is bounded on the west by southern spurs from the giant mountain regions of Eastern Tibet, that stretch their long arms in parallel ranges through Burma and Western Yunnan, and whose snow-clad crests send forth the great rivers Salween and Mekong to the south, the Yangtze and Yellow Rivers to the east, to fertilize the most productive regions on the surface of the globe.

It is this conformation that has so far presented an insurmountable barrier to the construction of a railway from Bhamo in Burmese territory to the high plateau of Yunnan, from whence the province of Szechwan, richest of all the eighteen provinces in agricultural and mineral wealth, could be reached. Some day the coal, iron, gold, oil, and salt of Szechwan will be exploited, and future generations may find in the millionaires of Szechwan Chinese speculators as able and far-seeing as the financial magnates who now practically control the destinies of millions in the Western world.

The portion south of the Yangtze is hilly rather than mountainous, and the eastern portion north of that great river is a vast plain of rich soil, through which the Yellow River, which from its periodical inundations is called China's Sorrow, flows for over five hundred miles.

In a country so vast, internal means of communication are of the first importance, and here China enjoys natural facilities unequalled by any area of similar extent. Three great rivers flow eastward and southward — the Hoang-ho, or Yellow River, in the north, the Yangtze in the centre, and the Pearl River, of which the West River is the largest branch, in the south. The Yangtze alone with its affluents is calculated to afford no less than 36,000 miles of waterways. The river population of China comprises many millions, whose varied occupations present some of the most interesting aspects of Chinese life.

The population of China is composed of different tribes or clans, whose records date back to the dynasty of Fuh-hi, 2800 B.C. Sometimes divided in separate kingdoms, sometimes united by waves of conquest, the northern portion was welded into one empire by the conqueror, Ghengis Khan, in A.D. 1234, and seventy years later the southern portion was added by his son, Kublai Khan, who overthrew the Sung dynasty. It was during his reign that China was visited by Marco Polo, from the records of whose travels we find that even at that time the financial system of the Far East was so far advanced that paper money was used by the Chinese, while in the city of Cambaluc — the Peking of to-

CHAPTER I

day — Christian, Saracen, and Chinese astrologers consulted an astrolabe to forecast the nature of the weather, thus anticipating the meteorological bureaux of to-day.

There are, however, still districts in the southern portion of China where the aboriginal inhabitants have never accepted the position of complete incorporation with the Chinese neighbours. In the mountain district between the provinces of Kwangtung and Hunan a tribe exists known as the Yu people, in whose territory no Chinese officials are permitted to reside, nor do they allow strangers to enter their towns, which are built on crags difficult of access and capable of offering a stubborn resistance to attack. Their chief occupation is forestry, the timber being cut during the winter and floated down the mountain streams when in flood. Their customs are peculiar. Among them is the vendetta, which is practised by the Yu alone of all the people in the Far East. But no woman is ever injured; and even during the fiercest fighting the women can continue their work in the fields with safety. Their original home was in Yunnan and the western part of Kwangsi, from whence they were driven out by the Chinese in the time of the Sung dynasty. The Yu, Lolos, Miao-tse, Sy-fans, etc. (all Chinese names expressive of contempt, like our "barbarians"), are stated by Ma-tonan-lin and other Chinese historians to have been found inhabiting the country when, six thousand years ago, it was occupied by the ancestors of the Chinese, who came from the north-west. The savage inhabitants were gradually driven into the hills, where their descendants are still found. Their traditions point to their having been cannibals. Intermarriage with the Chinese is very rare, the

Chinese regarding such a union as a *mésalliance*, and the aboriginal peoples as a cowardly desertion to the enemy. The embroideries worked by the women are different from those of the Chinese and, I am informed, more resemble the embroideries now worked at Bethlehem. They are worked on dark cloth in red, or sometimes red and yellow.

After the time of Kublai Khan, succeeding centuries found the various divisions of the Chinese again disunited, in accordance with a very old Chinese proverb frequently heard at the present day, "Long united we divide: long divided we unite"; but the final welding took place under Shun-chi, who established the Tsing dynasty in 1644, and imposed upon all Chinese people, as a permanent and evident mark of subjection, the shaving of the front portion of the head and braiding of the back hair into a queue after the Tartar fashion — an order at first resented bitterly, but afterwards acquiesced in as an old custom. To this day the removal of the queue and allowing the hair to grow on the front portion of the head is regarded as a casting off of allegiance to the dynasty. In the Taiping rebellion that raged in the southern provinces from 1850 to 1867, and which down to its suppression by Gordon and Li Hung Chang is computed to have cost the lives of twenty-two and a half millions of people, the removal of the queue and allowing the hair to grow freely was the symbol adopted by the rebels.

To secure the empire against future risings, the Manchu conquerors placed Tartar garrisons in every great city, where separate quarters were allotted to them, and for two hundred and sixty years these so-called Tartar soldiers and their families have been supported with doles of rice. They were not allowed to trade, nor to intermarry with the Chinese. The consequence was inevitable. They have become an idle population in whom the qualities of the old virile Manchus have deteriorated, and supply a large proportion of the elements of disorder and violence. Of late, the prohibition against entering into business and intermarrying with the Chinese has been removed, and they will ultimately be absorbed into the general population.

From the point of view of a trained soldier these Tartar "troops" were no more than armed rabble, with the most primitive ideas of military movements; but in the north the exigencies of the situation have compelled the adoption of Western drill, adding immensely to the efficiency but sadly diminishing the picturesqueness of the armies — for there is no homogeneous territorial army, each province supplying its own independent force, the goodness or badness of which depends upon the energy and ability of the viceroy.

The pay of a Chinese soldier is ostensibly about six dollars a month, which would be quite sufficient for his support were it not reduced to about half that amount by the squeezes of the officers and non-commissioned officers through whose hands it passes. He receives also one hundred pounds of rice, which is not always palatable, the weight being made up by an admixture of sand and mud to replace the "squeeze" by the various hands through which the rice tribute has passed.

While under arms he is clothed in a short Chinese jacket of

scarlet, blue, or black, on the front and back of which are the name and symbol of his regiment. The sleeves are wide and the arms have free play. The shape of the hat varies in every corps, the small round Chinese hat being sometimes worn, or a peakless cap, while some regiments wear immense straw hats, which hang on the back except when the sun is unduly hot. The trousers are dark blue of the usual Chinese pattern, tied round the ankles. The costume is not unsoldierlike, and when in mass the effect is strikingly picturesque; but it must not be inferred that all the men on a large parade are drilled soldiers. An order to the officer commanding to parade his corps for inspection not seldom interferes seriously with the labour force of the day. He draws the daily pay of, say, two thousand men, but his average muster may not exceed three hundred. This is a kind of gambling with Fortune at which China is disposed to wink as being merely a somewhat undue extension of the principle of squeeze that is the warp and woof of every Chinese employee, public or private. But he must not be found out; therefore seventeen hundred coolies are collected by hook or by crook, and duly attired in uniform, possibly being shown how to handle their rifles at the salute. The muster over, the coolies return to their work, and the arms and uniform are replaced in store until the next occasion.

The officers are chosen from the better classes, except when a more than usually ferocious robber is captured, when sometimes his supposed bravery is utilized by giving him an army command. The young officers undergo some kind of elementary training. In Canton it was until lately the custom to have an annual examination of their proficiency in riding and archery. In a field outside the city a curved trench about five feet wide and two feet deep was cut for about two hundred and fifty yards. At intervals of fifty yards were erected close to the trench three pillars of soft material each six feet high by two feet in diameter. Into each of these pillars the candidate, who was mounted on a small pony and seated in a saddle to fall out of which would require an active effort, was required to shoot an arrow as he passed at a gallop. With bow ready strung and two spare arrows in his girdle, he was started to gallop along the trench that was palpably dug to prevent the ponies from swerving, as the reins were flung upon his neck. As the candidate passed within two or three feet of the pillar targets the feat would not appear to have been difficult. If all three arrows were successfully planted the candidate was at the end of the course received with applause, and his name favourably noted by the mandarins, who sat in state in an open pavilion close by. But this description would not at present apply to the northern provinces, where some of the armies are apparently as well drilled, armed, and turned out as European troops. That Chinese troops are not wanting in bravery has been proved; and if properly led a Chinese drilled army of to-day might prove as formidable as were the hosts of Ghengis Khan, when in the thirteenth century they swept over Western Asia and into Europe as far as Budapest.

It has been stated that the empire has been welded together by its conquerors, but perhaps it would be more correct to say that it coheres by the almost universal acceptance of the ethics of Confucius, whose wise precepts — delivered five hundred years before the birth of Christ — inculcated all the cardinal virtues, and included love and respect for parents; respect for the Prince; respect for and obedience to superiors; respect for age, and courteous manners towards all. He held that at their birth all men were by nature radically good, but "as gems unwrought serve no useful end, so men untaught will never know what right conduct is."

The bedrock upon which the stability of China has rested for over two thousand years is the family life, the patriarchal system reaching upwards in ever-widening circles, from the hut of the peasant to the palace of the Sovereign. The house is ruled by the parents, the village by the elders, after which the officials step in, and the districts are governed by mandarins, whose rank of magistrate, prefect, taotai, governor, or viceroy indicate the importance of the areas over which they rule, each acting on principles settled by ancient custom, but with wide latitude in the carrying out of details. Nothing is more charming in respectable Chinese families than the reverential respect of children for their parents, and this respect is responded to by great affection for the children. It is a very pretty sight to see a young child enter the room and gravely perform the kotow to his father and mother. No young man would dare to eat or drink in the presence of his father or mother until invited to do so. Among the princely families the etiquette is so rigid that if a son is addressed by his father while at table he must stand up before answering.

It is sometimes assumed that the custom of wealthy Chinese having two, three, or more "wives" must lead to much confusion in questions of inheritance, but there is no real difficulty in the matter, for although the custom allows the legalized connection with a plurality of wives, there is really but one legal wife acknowledged as being the head of the house. She is called the kit-fat, or first wife, and though she may be childless all the children born of the other "wives" are considered as being hers, and to her alone do the children pay the reverence due to a parent, their own mothers being considered as being in the position of aunts. Strange though it may appear to Western ideas, this position seems to be accepted by the associated wives with equanimity. The custom probably originated in the acknowledged necessity to have a son or sons to carry on the worship at the family ancestral hall, where the tablets of deceased members are preserved. Sometimes instead of taking to himself a plurality of wives a man adopts a son, who is thenceforth in the position of eldest son, and cannot be displaced, even though a wife should afterwards bear a son. A daughter is on a different plane. She is not supposed to be capable of carrying out the family worship, and cannot perpetuate the family name. A daughter, too, means a dower in days to come, so sometimes a father determines, if he has already a daughter, that no more shall be permitted to live. This determination is always taken before the birth of the infant daughter, the child in that case being immersed in a bucket of water at the instant of its birth, so that from the Chinese point of view it has never existed; but female children who have practically begun a separate existence are never destroyed. In such cases the father is quite as fond of the daughter as of the sons, and in families where tutors are engaged the girls pursue their studies with their brothers.

The power of the parents is practically unlimited, extending even to life or death. A mother might kill her son without fear of legal punishment, but if, in defending himself, he killed his parent, he would be put to death by the lin-chi — or death by a thousand cuts — a horrible punishment reserved for traitors, parricides, or husband murderers. Indeed, while theoretically the woman is in China considered inferior, the kit-fat, or principal wife, is really the controller of the family, including the wives of her sons. She rules the household with a rod of iron, and has considerable, if not a paramount, influence in the conduct of the family affairs. The wife of an official is entitled to wear the ornaments and insignia of her husband's rank, and in the Imperial Palace the Dowager-Empress of the day is probably the most important personage in the empire after the Emperor.

In a Hong Kong paper a short time ago there appeared a paragraph reciting that a wealthy young Chinese, whose mother controlled a large business in Canton, had been spending the money of the firm too lavishly, the attraction of motor-cars and other vehicles of extravagance being too powerful for him. After various endeavours to control him, the mother at length prepared chains and fetters, and had him locked up. He, however, escaped, and the irate mother announced her intention to exercise her maternal rights on his return by cutting the tendons of his ankles and thus crippling him. The account proceeded to say that this treatment is often resorted to by irate parents with prodigal sons.

The most incomprehensible custom among Chinese women

of family is that of foot-binding, which is generally begun at the age of three or four, the process being very slow. Gradually the toes, other than the great toe, are forced back under the sole, so that when the operation is complete the girl is only able to hobble about on the great toes. When a Chinese lady goes out, not using her sedan chair, she is either carried by a female slave pick-a-back, or walks supported on either side by two female attendants. Nevertheless, Chinese women of the humbler classes are sometimes to be seen working in the fields with bound feet. Why their mothers should have inflicted the torture upon them, or why, when they had come to years of discretion, they did not attempt to gradually unbind their feet, seems incomprehensible. The explanation is that not alone would the unbinding inflict as much torture, but slaves and their descendants are not permitted to bind the feet; the deformity is therefore a badge of a free and reputable family, and a girl with bound feet has a better prospect of being well married than her more comfortable and capable sister, upon whom no burden of artificial deformity has been placed. The origin of the custom is lost in the mists of antiquity. One would imagine that the example of the Imperial family ought to have had an effect in changing it, for the Manchu ladies do not bind their feet; but though several edicts have been issued forbidding it, the custom still continues. To Western eyes, bound feet are as great a deformity as is the tight-lacing of European ladies to the Chinese; but physically the former is much less injurious than the latter, which not alone deforms the skeleton, but displaces almost every one of the internal organs.

CHAPTER II

The marriages are arranged in a somewhat similar manner to that of the Irish peasants. The negotiations are usually begun by a go-between instructed by the young man's family, the etiquette of the entire proceeding being rigidly adhered to. There is one insurmountable objection to unrestricted choice — the bridegroom and bride must not bear the same name, except in the province of Honan, where the prohibition is disregarded. The extent of this restriction will be realized when we remember that among the four hundred millions of Chinese there are not much over a hundred family names. There may be four millions of Wongs, but no man of that name may marry any one of the four millions. As marriage is the principal event of a Chinese woman's life, she has crowded into it as much gorgeous ceremonial as the circumstances of her parents will allow. The day before she leaves her ancestral home her trousseau and presents are forwarded to her new home. At the wedding of a daughter of a wealthy gentleman in Canton a few years ago, seven hundred coolies were engaged in transporting in procession all these belongings, some of the presents being of great beauty and value. The next day the bridegroom arrived with his procession of two hundred men — some on horseback, some armed and in military array — trays of sweetmeats, and numbers of children representing good fairies. The inevitable red lanterns,

CHAPTER II

with a band, led the procession, which was brought up by a dragon thirty feet long, the legs being supplied by boys, who carried their portion on sticks, and jumping up and down gave life and motion to the monster.

The bridal chair in which the bride was carried was elaborately carved and decorated. Its colour was red, picked out with blue feathers of the kingfisher carefully gummed on, which has the effect of enamel. On arrival at her new home, the bride was met with the usual ceremonies, and was carried over the threshold on which was a fire lighted in a pan, lest she should by any chance be accompanied by evil influences.

This carrying of the bride over the threshold is sometimes practised in the Highlands of Scotland, the ceremony having been observed when Her Royal Highness Princess Louise, Duchess of Argyll, first entered Inveraray Castle as a bride.

The day after the wedding it is the custom for the bride to cook her husband's rice, the fire being made from wood, which forms part of her trousseau, as she is supposed to bring everything necessary for the purpose to her new home. At a wedding at Macao not long ago, on proceeding to perform the usual ceremony, it was found to the consternation of the bride that no firewood had been sent. Her mother-in-law good-naturedly offered to give her the wood, but this the proud bride would by no means permit. Calling her amah, she directed her to fetch two rolls of silk, each worth about forty dollars, and with them she cooked the rice. When next her father came to see her she told him of the occurrence. He said, "You did right, my daughter; you have saved your father's face";

and on his return he promptly dispatched a hundred coolies laden with firewood, which was more than the bridegroom's house could hold.

The ceremony of the "teasing of the bride" is sometimes trying for her, but in good families propriety is rarely outraged. Here is an account of such a ceremony which took place in the house of one of our friends the day after her marriage. The ladies' dinner was over when we arrived; the gentlemen had not yet come up from their dinner at the restaurant. This evening the bride had gone round the tables pouring out samshu, a ceremony that her mother-in-law had performed on the previous evening. The bride came into the room wearing a gorgeous and elaborate costume of red, the long ribbon-like arrangements over her skirt, huge open-work collar of red and gold, and the bridal crown on her head. The veil of pearls was looped back from her face, and she looked arch and smiling. It was quite a relief to see her after the shrinking, downcast girl of the previous evening. When the gentlemen came the "teasing" of the bride began. She was given various puzzles to solve, two or three of which she undid very deftly. An intricate Japanese puzzle was produced, but the mother-in-law would not allow it to be given to the bride to solve, as she said it was too difficult. The bridegroom came in, and the gentlemen present demanded that he and the bride should walk round the room together, which they did, and were then made to repeat the peregrination. There was a demand that the pearl veil, which had been let down, should be hooked back that all present might see her face. This was done. Then a sort of poetic category was put to her, a gentleman of the family standing near to judge if she answered correctly. The bride was told to ask her husband to take her hand; to ask him what he had gained in marrying her, and so on. The bride had to go round the room saluting and offering tea to the various gentlemen. To one or two relatives she kotowed, and one or two kotowed to her. This, of course, was a question of seniority. Some of the questions and remarks made on the bride must have been trying and unpleasant to any young lady, but being in Chinese they were incomprehensible to us. The idea of the custom is to test the temper, character, and cleverness of the bride.

In the case of people of the lower orders, the ceremony must be more than unpleasant, as there is sometimes rough horseplay, the unfortunate bride being insulted, and now and again pinched severely. But she must show no display of temper or resentment at the rough process, as it would be taken as an indication that she did not possess the qualification of non-resisting submission to her husband.

Each family possesses an ancestral "hall," where are kept the tablets of every defunct member of the family, before which incense sticks are burnt daily, and where once or twice a year all the members of the family within reach attend to lay offerings before the tablets in a spirit of reverence. Should a man disgrace his family he is often repudiated as a member, and at his death no tablet will be placed for him in the ancestral hall. The consequence is that his descendants cannot present themselves for the competitive examinations upon which all official position depends.

The family lands are apportioned annually, and from one

particular portion the contribution must be paid towards the expenses of the local temple, including the theatrical performances that cost considerable sums. This portion of the family land is cultivated by each member of the family in turn. If the tenant be a Christian he declines to pay the money for purposes to which he claims to have a conscientious objection. Increased expense therefore falls upon the other members of the family, who feel that the secession has placed an additional burden upon them. The result is a feeling of antagonism to Christianity; otherwise religious intolerance is not characteristic of the Chinese.

The official hierarchy in China is peculiarly constituted. China is, like all democracies, intensely autocratic, and, within certain bounds, each official is a law unto himself. To become an official is therefore the ambition of every clever boy. At the triennial examinations held in the capitals of provinces, from 150,000 to 200,000 candidates present themselves, who have passed successfully preliminary competitive examinations held annually at various places. To compete in these examinations a certificate must be produced by the candidate that he is a member of a known family. If unsuccessful, he may go on competing at every triennial examination held during his life. Here we see the importance of family tablets in the ancestral hall. No barber, or actor, or member of the boat population may compete.

At Canton, and also at Nanking and other great cities, may be seen the examination halls and the rows of cells in which the candidates — after being rigidly searched to ensure that no scrap of paper or writing is retained that could assist them in the tremendous pending effort of memory — are strictly confined during the time that the examinations last. In Canton there are over eleven thousand; in Nanking there are many more. The lean-to cells are built in rows, and measure three feet eight inches in width by five feet nine inches in length, being six feet high in front and nine feet in the back. From this cell the candidate may not stir, except as an acknowledgment of failure, and many die during the trial. At Nanking during an examination an average of twenty-five deaths occurred daily.

Those who win the prizes are at once appointed to office, and are received at their homes with great honour. Of those who have passed lower down, some are allocated to different provinces, where they remain in waiting at the expense of the viceroy until some situation becomes vacant. Once appointed they are eligible for promotion to the position of prefect or taotai, or governor, or even viceroy. In all these promotions money plays no inconsiderable part, and a wealthy man may purchase mandarin's rank without the drudgery of examination, as is not unknown in countries that boast of more advanced civilization. In some cases, if a boy shows great intelligence and aptitude for learning, a syndicate is formed by his family, and no expense is spared upon his education. Should he be successful and attain a position of importance, his family rise with him in wealth and influence, and the syndicate turns out a productive speculation. The whole system of examination is one of cramming, which, with competitive examinations, was adopted by England from the Chinese.

The Chinaman who has passed the examination and received

what we colloquially term his B.A. degree, even though he obtains no official employment, holds himself above all manual labour, and however poor he may be he belongs thereafter to the body of *literati* known as the gentry, who are consulted on all matters affecting the district in which they reside. It is not easy to know how they live, but the Chinese, like all Easterns, have a great respect for men of letters, and have not yet become so civilized as to abandon higher ideals for the degrading worship of wealth. There is probably found for such men suitable employment in their localities that works into the social economy. There are, of course, among them some lazy ones who, for want of regular work, abandon themselves to the solace of opium-smoking; but the class is a valuable leaven in the mass of the population.

The viceroy of a province is really semi-independent. His nominal salary in a province of possibly sixty millions of inhabitants is £1000 or £2000 a year, out of which he must supply an army, possibly a navy, internal customs, and civil service.

The taxes are very much at his discretion, with the exception of the settled duty paid by the cultivators on seed corn, that being the way in which the land tax is levied. That paid, the small cultivator is practically free from official interference, and such a man in China if quiet and honest is as free as any man of his position elsewhere.

This method of levying a land tax is most ingenious, and has existed from time immemorial. The land is taxed, not proportionate to its area, but to its productive capacity. Of two plots of equal area one may produce a return from two bushels, while the other being

CHAPTER II

poorer soil will require wider sowing and take but one bushel. All seed must be procured through the official, who levies an equal rate upon it. The same idea governs the computation of distance. A road to the top of a hill may be counted and carriage paid for ten li, the return down hill being measured as five or six, it being assumed that the muscular exertion and time are in both cases being paid for at the same rate.

There are, besides the seed tax, likin, or internal customs, levied on transport of all commodities between districts, and various imposts upon traders. When a man has amassed any wealth he is bled pretty freely. Should a loan be requested it could only be refused at a risk that he would not care to face, and any idea of its repayment is out of the question. But should the demands exceed the bounds of custom there is a check. The people of all classes know pretty well how far the cord may be drawn before it breaks. Should the demands be excessive the people put up their shutters, refusing to do any business, and memorial the Throne. Should such a state of affairs continue for any time even a viceroy would be recalled. Such a state of affairs existed a few years ago in Canton over a proposal to collect a new tax. The people resisted, and at length the viceroy yielded.

The principles on which the viceroy acts are adopted in a lesser degree by all officials, but the people seem to understand the custom and accept it, and in the ordinary business of life justice is on the whole administered satisfactorily.

There are, of course, exceptions. In the province of Kwangtung the house of a well-to-do man living in the country was attacked by a numerous band of armed robbers. The owner stoutly defended his house and having killed three of the assailants the robbers decamped. But this was not the end of it, for the indignant robbers lodged a complaint with the magistrate, who summoned the owner of the assailed house to appear, which he did with fear and trembling. He was obliged to pay a hundred and fifty dollars before he was admitted to the presence of the magistrate, who, instead of commending him for his bravery, scolded him roundly, and ordered him to pay the funeral expenses of the three dead robbers. The system of payments to everybody connected with the court, from the judge downwards, would appear to be destructive of every principle of justice; but a highly educated Chinese official, who held the degree of a Scotch university and who had experience of the colony of Hong Kong, when speaking on the subject, declared that he would rather have a case tried in a Chinese court than in a British, for while he knew what he would pay in the first, in the colonial court the lawyers would not let him off while he had a dollar to spend.

When the territory of Kowloon was leased from China and added to the colony of Hong Kong (after some armed resistance by the inhabitants, who had been led to believe that with the change of the flag terrible things would happen to them), local courts were established giving summary jurisdiction to their head-men sitting with a British magistrate, but a proviso was inserted that no lawyer or solicitor should practise in these courts. The result was peaceful settlement of disputes, generally by the arbitration of the British magistrate, at the joint request of both parties to the dispute.

CHAPTER II

The punishments inflicted in Chinese courts are severe, and sometimes very terrible. The ordinary punishment for minor offences is the cangue and the bastinado. The cangue is a three-inch board about three feet square, with a hole in the centre for the neck. When this is padlocked on the neck of the culprit he is placed outside the door of the court, with his offence written upon the cangue, or is sometimes allowed to walk through the town. In this position he cannot feed himself, as his hands cannot reach his head, nor can he lie down or rest in comfort. Sometimes the hands are fastened to the cangue. The punishment is more severe than that of our old parish stocks, but the idea is the same. Were it in the power of a troublesome fly to irritate a Chinaman, which it is not, he might suffer grave discomfort if the insects were active.

The bastinado is a different matter. This is administered by placing the prisoner on his face, his feet being held by one man and his head by another. The blows are inflicted with a large bamboo or with two small ones. The large bamboo looks more formidable, but though the strokes are heavy they break no bones, and do but little injury. The small bamboos are used in a different manner. Taking one in each hand, the operator sits down and strikes the culprit rapidly with alternate strokes, apparently mere taps. These are hardly felt for the first fifty or sixty taps, and the skin is not broken; but after this phase the flesh below the skin becomes regularly broken up, and the agony is very great. The recovery from this severe punishment is slow, as the tissues are destroyed for the time being.

These are, however, the light punishments; torture for the

purpose of extracting evidence is still inflicted, and in pursuance of a custom that down to a late period had acquired the force of a law, that no person should be executed except he had confessed his crime, the palpable difficulty of that apparently beneficent rule was surmounted by the administration of torture, until the victim was reduced to such a state of mutilation and despair that he was prepared to state anything that would secure for him relief from his sufferings by a speedy death. It must be acknowledged that the pressure of the torture has now and again secured valuable evidence from unwilling witnesses that may have been capable of independent proof, but as a rule such evidence was utterly untrustworthy.

The following story was told to me by a Chinese gentleman who had personal knowledge of some of the persons concerned.

A son and daughter of two wealthy families were married. At the conclusion of the first evening's ceremonies the bride and bridegroom retired to their apartments, which were separated from the main house. Some time after they had retired, hearing a noise overhead, the bridegroom got up and putting on his red bridal dress he lit a candle and went up to the loft. Here he found a robber, who had entered through a hole in the roof, and who, seeing himself detected, after a short struggle plunged a knife into the bridegroom and killed him. He then assumed the bridegroom's dress, and taking the candle in his hand he boldly went down to the chamber where the bride awaited the return of her husband. As Chinese brides do not see their husbands before marriage, and as she was somewhat agitated, she did not perceive that the robber was not her newly married spouse. He told her that he had found that a robber had entered the house, but had made his escape on his appearance. He then said that as there were robbers the bride had better hand her jewels to him, and he would take them to his father's apartments and place them in the safe. This she did, handing over jewels to the value of several thousand taels. The robber walked out, and he and the jewels disappeared.

Early next morning the father of the bridegroom came to visit his son, and on entering the apartment was told by the bride that she had not seen her husband since he took the jewels to have them deposited in safe keeping. The father on hearing the story went up to the loft, where he found the dead body of his son. He searched about and in one of the courtyards outside he found a strange shoe.

For the wedding a number of the friends of the family had assembled who were, as usual, accommodated in the house. Among them was a young man, a B.A., and most respectably connected. The father taking the strange shoe went round all the guests, who had just arisen. On comparing the shoe he found that it belonged to the young B.A., who was wearing its fellow, the other shoe being that of his murdered son. The father was a cautious man, so instead of taking immediate action he returned to the young widow and questioned her closely. He asked if she could identify the man whom she had mistaken for her husband. She said that she could not. He begged her to think if there was any mark by which identification was possible, and after thinking for a time she answered "Yes," that she now remembered having remarked that he had lost a thumb. The father returned to the guest chamber and asked the B.A. for explanation of his wearing the son's shoe, for which he accounted by the statement that having occasion to go out during the night he had stumbled in crossing one of the courtyards and lost his shoe in the dark, and groping about had found and put on what he thought was his own. Upon examining his hands he was found to be minus a thumb. The father having no further doubt caused him to be forthwith arrested and taken before the prefect. The young man denied all knowledge of the murder, saying that he had a wife and child, was well off, and was a friend of the murdered bridegroom. He was put to the torture and under its pressure he confessed that he was the murderer. The body had been examined and the extent of the wound carefully measured and noted. Asked to say how he had disposed of the knife with which the murder had been committed, and what had become of the jewels, he professed his inability to say, though tortured to the last extremity. He was then beheaded. His uncle, however, and his widow would not believe in his guilt, and they presented to all the superior authorities in turn petitions against the action of the prefect, who ought not to have ordered the execution until corroborative proof of the confession had been secured by the production of the knife and the jewels, but the officials refused to listen to them. At length they appealed to the viceroy, who, seeing their persistence, concluded that there must be something in a belief that braved the gravest punishment by petitioning against a mandarin of prefect rank. He sent for the father and widow of the murdered man, who repeated the story, which seemed almost conclusive evidence of the young man's guilt. He asked the widow

CHAPTER II

if she remembered from which hand the thumb was missing of the robber to whom she had given the jewels. She replied, "Yes, perfectly. It was the right." He then sent for the petitioning widow and asked her from which hand her husband had lost a thumb. She answered, "The left." Then recalling the father of the murdered man he bade him try to recollect if he had ever known any other man wanting a thumb. He said that there was such a man, a servant of his whom two years before he had dismissed for misconduct. Asked if he had noticed the dismissed man during the time of the wedding the answer was that he had, but he had not seen him since.

The viceroy then had inquiry made, and the man was traced to another province, where he was living in affluence, with a good shop, etc. He was arrested, and under torture confessed the crime and told where he had concealed the knife and disposed of the jewels. The knife had a wide blade that coincided with the width of the wound, and a portion of the jewels were recovered, some having been pawned, some sold. The prefect was degraded and punished for culpable want of due care in having executed the man without securing complete proof by the production of the knife and the jewels.

The case is curious as showing the danger that lurks in all cases of circumstantial evidence, and also, from a purely utilitarian point of view, the failure and success of the system of torture. It will always be to me a source of deep gratification that during my administration of the government of Hong Kong, in the case of two murderers surrendered from that colony and convicted after a fair trial and on reliable evidence, I induced the then viceroy to break through the immemorial custom, and have the criminals executed without the previous application of torture, though they refused to confess to the last. The precedent once made, this survival of barbarous times will no longer operate in cases of culprits surrendered from under the folds of the Union Jack, and awakening China may, I hope, in such matters of criminal practice soon find herself in line with the other civilized nations of the world, to the relief of cruel injustice and much human suffering.

CHAPTER III

In China the gradations of the social fabric as generally accepted are
- First. — The *literati*; for mind is superior to matter.
- Second. — The agriculturist; for he produces from the soil.
- Third. — The artisan; for he is a creator from the raw material.
- Fourth. — The merchant; for he is a distributor.
- Fifth. — The soldier; for he is but a destroyer.

However superficially logical this division is, the Chinese have failed to realize that the army is an insurance and protection, wanting which all other classes may be destroyed; but the fallacy has had an unfortunate influence upon China, for until within a few years the various so-called armies were simply hordes of undisciplined men, whose officers were, as I have before said, sometimes robbers reprieved on account of supposed courage and given command of so-called soldiers. But this is now changed, and such armies as those of Yuan Shi Kai and Chang Chi Tung (viceroy at Hankow) are well disciplined and officered. This viceroy adopted an effective method of combating the contempt with which the army was regarded by the *literati*. He established a naval and agricultural college, and colleges for the teaching of geography, history, and mathematics, and formed all the students into a cadet corps. When I was in Hankow the viceroy invited me to see his army of eight thousand men, who were then on maneuvres in the neighbourhood, and on my arrival I was received by a guard of honour of one hundred of these cadets, whose smart turn-out and soldierly appearance impressed me very favourably. They were well clothed and well armed, as indeed were all the troops, whom I had an opportunity of inspecting during the maneuvres under the guidance of a German captain in the viceroy's service, who was told off to accompany me. I have no doubt that many of those cadets are now officers, and will tend to raise the character of the army.

The importance of agriculture is emphasized by the annual ceremony of ploughing three furrows by the Emperor at the Temple of Agriculture in the presence of all the princes and high officials of Peking. Furrows are afterwards ploughed by the princes and the high officers of the Crown. Agriculture is the business of probably nine-tenths of the population, and in no country in the world is the fertility of the soil preserved more thoroughly. In the portions of China visited by me no idle land was to be seen, but everywhere the country smiled with great fields of grain or rape or vegetables, alternating with pollarded mulberry trees in the silk-producing districts, while extensive tracts of the beautiful pink or white lotuses are grown, the seeds of which as well as the tuberous roots are used for food and the large leaves for wrappers. Nothing in the shape of manure is lost in city, town, or village; everything goes at once back to the fields, and nowhere in China is a river polluted by the wasted wealth of city sewers. On the banks of the canals the cultivators even dredge up the mud and distribute it over their fields by various ingenious devices.

The rural population is arranged in village communities, each village having its own head-man and elders, to whom great respect is shown. Sometimes there is a feud between two villages over disputed boundaries or smaller matters, in which case, if the elders cannot arrange matters, the quarrel may develop into a fight in which many lives are lost. Nobody interferes and the matter is settled *vi et armis*.

But this absence of local government control has its drawbacks; for as sugar attracts ants, so unprotected wealth attracts robbers, and gang robberies are frequent, generally by armed men, who do not hesitate to add murder to robbery. Nor are these attacks confined to distant rural districts. Only a few months ago an attack was made upon a strongly built and fortified country house belonging to one of the wealthiest silk merchants in Canton, who had specially designed and built the house to resist attack, and had armed his retainers with repeating rifles. Twenty-five boats, containing about three hundred men, came up the river, and an attack was made at six p.m. that lasted for seven hours. At length the fortified door was blown in by dynamite and the house taken. Eighty thousand dollars' worth of valuables was carried off, and the owner and his two sons were carried away for ransom. Several of the retainers were killed and thirteen of the robbers.

The country people are very superstitious and dislike extremely any building or work that overlooks the villages, as they say that it has an unlucky effect upon their *fung sui*, a term that means literally wind and water, but may be translated freely as elemental forces. This superstitious feeling sometimes creates difficulty with engineers and others laying out railways or other works. The feeling is kept alive by the geomancers, whose mysterious business it is to discover and point out lucky positions for family graves, a body of an important person sometimes remaining unburied for years pending definite advice from the geomancer as to the best position for the grave, which is always made on a hill-side. They also arrange the lucky days for marriages, etc. When the telegraph was being laid between Hong Kong and Canton, the villagers at one point protested loudly against the erection of a pole in a particular position, as they were informed that it would interfere with the *fung sui* of the village. The engineer in charge, who fortunately knew his Chinese, did not attempt to oppose them; but taking out his binoculars he looked closely at the ground and said, "You are right; I am glad the geomancer pointed that out. It is not a favourable place." Then again apparently using the glasses, he examined long and carefully various points at which he had no intention of placing the pole. At length he came to a spot about twenty yards away, which suited him as well as the first, when after a lengthened examination he said, with an audible sigh of deep relief, "I am glad to find that this place is all right," and the pole was erected without further objection.

While gang robberies are frequent, there is not much petty theft, as in small towns the people appoint a local policeman, who is employed under a guarantee that if anything is stolen he pays the damage. In small matters this is effective.

The necessity for making villages secure against ordinary

attack is palpable, and many villages in country districts are surrounded by high walls that secure them from such attack. In some, guns of ancient pattern are mounted on the walls.

The prosperity of a town is shown by the number of pawnshops, which are always high towers solidly built and strongly fortified. The Chinese pawnshop differs from those of Western nations, as it is not merely a place for the advance of money upon goods deposited, but also the receptacle for all spare valuables. Few Chinese keep their winter clothing at home during summer, or vice versa. When the season changes the appropriate clothing is released, and that to be put by pawned in its place. This arrangement secures safe keeping, and if any balance remains in hand it is turned over commercially before the recurring season demands its use for the release of the pawned attire. Sometimes very valuable pieces of jewellery or porcelain remain on the hands of the pawnshop keeper, and interesting objects may from time to time be procurable from his store.

Next to agriculture in general importance is the fishing industry, in which many millions of the population are engaged, the river boat population forming a class apart, whose home is exclusively upon their boats. To describe the variety of boats of all kinds found in Chinese waters would require a volume. The tens of thousands of junks engaged in the coasting trade and on the great rivers vary from five to five hundred tons capacity, while every town upon ocean river or canal has its house boats, flower boats, or floating restaurants and music halls, passenger boats, fishing boats, trading boats, etc. On these boats the family lives from the cradle to the grave, and while the mother is working the infant may be seen sprawling about the boat, to which it is attached by a strong cord, while a gourd is tied to its back, so that if it goes overboard it may be kept afloat until retrieved by the anchoring cord. In Hong Kong, where it is computed that there are about thirty thousand boat people in the harbour, the infant is strapped to the mother's back while she sculls the boat, the child's head — unprotected in the blazing sun — wagging from side to side until one wonders that it does not fly off.

The large junks, with their great high sterns and bold curves, and with the setting sun glinting on their yellow sails of matting, are a sight to stir the soul of an artist. Many of these carry guns, as the dangers of gang robberies on shore are equalled by that of piracy on sea or river, the West River having the most evil reputation in this respect. The unwillingness of junks to carry lights at night, lest their position should invite piratical attack, adds to the dangers of collision, and necessitates extreme caution after sunset in navigating the southern coasts of China. These junks convey all the cargo from the coast and riverside towns to the treaty ports, through which all trade between China and foreign nations is exchanged. The high square stern affords accommodation for the crew, but no man dares to desecrate the bow by sitting down there. On one occasion when we went by canal to Hangchow we stopped at Haining to observe the incoming of the great bore that at the vernal equinox sweeps up the river from the bay, and affords one of the most striking sights in the world. While preparing to measure the height of the wave by fixing a marked pole to the bow of a junk

CHAPTER III

lying high and dry alongside, which was most civilly permitted by the junkowner, one of the gentlemen sat down on the bow, upon which the junkowner tore him away in a fury of passion and made violent signs to him to leave the ship. Our interpreter coming up at the moment heard from the irate junkman what had occurred. He pointed out that the bow was sacred to his guardian deity, and such an insult as sitting down on the place where his incense sticks were daily burnt was sure to bring bad luck, if not destruction. Explanations and apologies on the score of ignorance followed, and a coin completed the reconciliation. The origin of touching the cap to the quarter-deck on our ships originated in the same idea, the crucifix being carried at the stem in the brave days of old.

The great wave or bore that I have just mentioned formed about six miles out in the bay, and we heard the roar and saw the advancing wall of water ten minutes before it arrived. The curling wave in front was about ten feet high and swept past at the rate of fourteen miles an hour, but the vast mass of swirling sea that rose behind the advancing wall was a sight more grand than the rapids above Niagara. I measured accurately its velocity and height. In one minute the tide rose nine feet nine inches on the sea wall that runs northward from Haining for a hundred miles. It is seventeen feet high, splendidly built with cut stone, and with the heavy stones on top (four feet by one foot) dovetailed to each other by iron clamps, similar to those I afterwards saw at the end of the great wall of China, where it abuts on the sea at Shan-hai-kwan.

If the land is thoroughly cultivated the same may be said of the waters, for in sea, river, lake, or pond, wherever water rests or flows, there is no device that ingenuity can conceive that is not used for the capture of fish, which enters largely into the food of the people; and no cultivation is more intensive than pisciculture, a fishpond being more valuable than ten times its area of cultivated land. Sometimes the pond belongs to a village, and nothing comes amiss that may serve to feed the fish, from the grass round the borders of the pond to the droppings of the silkworms in silk-producing districts. In such cases the village latrine is generally built over the pond; it may, therefore, be understood that Europeans generally eschew the coarse pond fish and prefer fresh or salt sea fish. These pond fish grow very rapidly, and are taken by nets of all shapes and sizes. Sometimes a net forty feet square is suspended from bamboo shears and worked by ropes and pulleys, the net being lowered and after a short time, during which fish may be driven towards it, slowly raised, the fish remaining in the net, the edges of which leave the waters first. In ponds of large area forty or fifty men may be seen, each with a net twelve to fifteen feet square suspended from a bamboo pole, all fishing at the same time. The entire pond is gone over, and as the fish are kept on the move large numbers are thus taken. They are then if near a river placed in well boats and sent alive to market. During the summer months the bays around the coast are covered by thousands of these large square nets. A net sometimes eighty feet square is fastened at each corner to poles, long in proportion to the depth of the water, the other ends of which are anchored by heavy weights. The men who work the nets live in a hut built upon long poles similarly weighted, and securely stayed by cables anchored at the four cardinal points of the compass. From the hut platform the net is manipulated by a bridle rope worked by a windlass. When the net is raised the fish fall into a purse in the centre, from which they are removed by men who row under the now suspended net and allow the fish to drop from the purse into the boat. These nets are set up sometimes in nine to ten fathoms. I have never seen them used in any other bays than those on the coast of China, where, it may be observed incidentally, there is hardly any perceptible growth of seaweed, and one never perceives the smell of the sea or feels the smack of salt upon the lips, as we do on our coasts.

I have said that the devices for the capture of fish are endless, from the large nets just described to the small fish trap set in every trench or gap through which water flows. But they do not end here, for about Ichang, on the Yangtze, otters are trained to drive fish into the nets; and on the lakes and canals a not unusual sight is a boat or raft with eight cormorants, who at the word of command go overboard and dive in pursuit of the fish. Sometimes the bird is recalcitrant, but a few smart strokes on the water close beside it with a long bamboo sends the bird under at once. When a fish is caught and swallowed the cormorant is taken on board and being held over a basket the lower mandible is drawn down, when out pops the fish uninjured, the cormorant being prevented from swallowing its prey by a cord tied round the lower part of the neck.

But the most curious device for the capture of fish is practised on the Pearl and West Rivers, where one sees poor lepers seated in the stern of a long narrow canoe along the side of which is a hinged board painted white. This they turn over the side at an angle during the night, and the fish jumping on to it are dexterously jerked into the boat. In the Norwegian fjords, baskets are sometimes hung or nets fastened under the splashes of whitewash marking the position of rings let into the rocky cliff where the yachts may tie up in an adverse wind. The fish jumping at the white mark, which possibly they mistake for a waterfall, are caught in the net or basket suspended below.

The boat population of the inland waters are liable to the same dangers from armed robbery as are their brothers on land, for the river pirates are a constant source of trouble. Even the large river steamers of the American pattern plying on the West River under the command of European officers are not always safe, though great precautions are taken, as the robbers sometimes embark as passengers if they know of any specie or valuables being on board, and at a given point produce revolvers and hold up the captain and crew, carrying off their booty in a confederate boat. On this account launches are not permitted to tow lighters with passengers alongside lest they should step on board, and in all large steamers the lower deck used by Chinese is separated from the upper by a companion-way with iron railings and locked door, or with an armed sentry standing beside it. About six years ago two stern-wheel passenger boats left Hong Kong for the West River one evening, to enter which the course was usedly laid north of Lintin, an island in the estuary of the Pearl River. The leading boat number one for some reason took a course to the south of Lintin, whereupon the captain of number two came to the conclusion that she was being pirated, so changing his course and blowing his whistle loudly he pressed on with a full head of steam and opened fire upon number one with rifles. Number one returned the fire, assuming that number two had been pirated and was attacking him. He steered back to Hong Kong and made a running fight, a hot fire being maintained until the boats had actually entered the harbour, when they were met by a police launch and the mistake was discovered. Over three hundred shots were fired, but happily nobody was hit. It is not a year since a train of seven or eight house-boats, full of passengers and towed by a steam launch that plies between Hangchow and Suchow on the Grand Canal, was held up by river pirates, who rifled the train as American trains are now and again held up in the Western States of America. These evidences of lawlessness are only the natural consequences of the neglect of the primary duty of a government to make effective police arrangements for the due protection of life and property, for Chinese under proper control are naturally law-abiding and peaceable. The Chinese system does not contemplate any police arrangements outside the principal cities. The small village communities arrange their own police, but there is no official means of combating the more serious offences short of a military expedition. The salutary principle of prevention is ignored and the fitful efforts of government devoted to punishment. This system doubtless acts as a deterrent when the punishment follows the crime so frequently as to impress upon evildoers the sense of its probability. Therefore it is that a strong viceroy makes a quiet province. When pointing out to Li Hung Chang the advisability of controlling a town well known as a headquarters of pirates, his

Excellency answered quietly, "We will exterminate them." He ruled the province of the two Kwangs with a rod of iron, and left Canton to the profound regret of every man who had property exposed to attack.

Li Hung Chang was the most able of the many able officials of China. He was supposed to have had strong Russian sympathies, but had he been in Tientsin or Peking instead of Canton when the Boxer trouble was brewing, it is probable that the dangerous conspiracy would never have been allowed to come to a head. The viceroys at Nanking and Hankow maintained peace in their provinces, though the "big knife" movement had its origin in their districts, and Li Hung Chang was as strong a man as either, or stronger. When he left Canton to try to reach Peking it was too late, and the issue had been joined between the Chinese Court and the foreign Powers. He would have done better had he remained in the turbulent southern province that he had ruled so sternly and efficiently. Dangerous as was the Boxer movement, it showed clearly the want of cohesion between the different portions of the Chinese empire. When the trouble broke out in the north, there were a large number of Cantonese students at Tientsin College, whose lives were as unsafe as if they were foreigners. Some Chinese gentlemen waited upon me on the subject. They were in great distress, as they had no means of getting their sons away. They begged me to endeavour to get the young men sent down by the British Consul, and undertook to pay any amount up to ten thousand dollars for the expense of chartering a ship. I telegraphed, guaranteeing the amount, to the British Consul, who kindly chartered a ship for the transit of the young men. The bill of over nine thousand dollars was at once paid by the Chinese gentlemen who had requested my good offices.

The fact is that between different provinces, speaking different patois, there exists in many cases a settled antipathy that has been handed down from the feuds and wars of bygone centuries. To this day the junks from Swatow land their cargoes in Hong Kong at a wharf where Swatow coolies are employed; did they land it at a wharf worked by Cantonese, there would certainly be disorder, and possibly fighting, before the discharge of the cargo.

The traveller in China is impressed with the vastness of its extent, the fertility of its various countries, the grandeur of its rivers, the beauty and boldness of its bridges, the strength of its city walls, the contrast of wealth and squalor in the cities, the untiring industry of the people. A more detailed knowledge compels admiration for their proficiency in arts and crafts.

A journey up the West River leads through the gorges, which gives one an idea of the teeming life of the Chinese water world. The West River is, next to the Yangtze, the one most often coming under the notice of foreigners, for the river is the principal scene of piratical attacks. Indeed, no native boat known to have valuable property on board was, some years ago, safe from attack if it did not pay blackmail, and carry a small flag indicating that it had done so. Perhaps the most curious craft on the river is the sternwheel boats, worked by man power. Sixteen coolies work the wheel after the manner of a treadmill, four more standing by as a relief. The work is very hard, and coolies engaged in this occupation do not live long; but in China that is a consideration that does not count, either with workman or master. Rafts float slowly down the yellow waters of the broad river-rafts three to four hundred yards long, with the "navigators" comfortably encamped; great junks, with their most picturesque fan-shaped sails; at every town a crowd of "slipper" boats, as sampans are called, which have a movable hood over the forepart, under which passengers sit. At Sam-shui, the principal station of the Imperial Customs in the river, a dragon-boat shoots out with twelve men. In it are carried a large red umbrella and a green flag, the umbrella being a symbol of honour, while around the sides are painted the honorific titles of the owner or person to whom it is dedicated. From here comes the matting made at Taiking that is sold by retail at ten dollars for a roll of forty yards.

Beyond Kwongli Island the gorges begin, through which the West River debouches on the plains on its journey to the sea. From the island one hundred and fifty acute sugar-loaf summits can be counted, and the tortuous gorges wind past a succession of steep valleys that must have been scored out when the mountain range was upheaved at a period of very great torrential rains.

Above the gorges the old town of Sui-hing is rather featureless, but is a landing-place for the Buddhist monasteries, built at various elevations on the precipitous sides of seven masses of white marble rising from the plain and called the Seven Stars. These old monasteries here and elsewhere are marvellously picturesque, perched as they usually are in situations that can only be reached by steep climbing. The temple is at the base of the cliff, and contains fine bronze figures of Kunyam, the goddess of mercy, with two guardians in bronze at her side. The figures are about ten feet high, and are supposed to be over one thousand years old. There is also a bronze bell said to be of still older date.

Through a great cave and up marble steps the marble temple is approached in which is a seated figure of the Queen of Heaven. The sculptured figure, like the temple itself, is hewn from the solid rock, the statue of the Queen of Heaven being in a shrine close by an opening through which the light strikes upon the well carved statue and drapery of white marble with a fine effect. The country round the Seven Stars is perfectly flat, and devoted to the growth of rice, fish, and lotus plants. In a large pond beneath the temple a water buffalo is feeding on the floating leaves of lilies, while its calf calmly swims beside the mother, now and again resting its head upon her quarter. One realizes how large a part the water buffalo plays in Chinese economy, for without it the cultivation of rice would be seriously curtailed. The buffalo ploughs the inundated field, wading in the mud literally up to its belly, when no other animal could draw the primitive plough through the deep mud. In the town of Sui-hing excellent pewter work is made, and here also are fashioned various articles from the white marble of the Seven Stars, the carving of which shows excellent workmanship.

West of Sui-hing lies the city of Wuchow, where the Fu-ho River joins the West River. Once a suspension bridge existed over the Fu-ho, and two cast-iron pillars about nine feet high and twelve inches in diameter are still standing, and have stood for several centuries. The pillars have both been welded at about four feet from the ground. I do not know if cast-iron can now be welded; if not, it is a lost art that certainly was known to the Chinese.

Below Wuchow, on the right bank of the river, is a district that will one day attract the big game sportsman. Here the tigers are so plentiful and so dangerous that the inhabitants do not dare to leave their homes after four or five o'clock in the afternoon. Farther down, on the left bank, is one of the most important Buddhist monasteries in China — Howlick — which accommodates about two hundred monks, and can take in an equal number of guests, who at certain seasons retire to the monastery for rest and reflection. It is situated about two miles from the river at an elevation of fifteen hundred feet. Approached by a steep pathway, at the entrance of which stand or sit two grey-robed monks armed with spears so as to be able to repel bad characters, and which as it approaches the monastery is formed into long flights of steps, Howlick is built upon a terraced plateau in the midst of primeval forest and close by a most picturesque gorge. The monastery is the resort of a large number of pilgrims, and Buddhist services take place daily in the temple, which, unlike most temples in China, is perfectly clean and well appointed. When I visited it the service was being intoned in strophe and antistrophe, the chanters at each recurrent verse kneeling and touching the ground with their foreheads. The only accompaniment was drums and gongs, the time being marked by tapping a wooden drum of the Buddhist shape, but all was very subdued. One monk played two or three gongs of different sizes, one being only about six inches in diameter. The two long tables on which the books of the readers were placed were loaded with cakes and fruit. The fronts were hung with rich embroideries. Such a service is paid for by the pilgrims, who receive the food placed upon the tables and distribute it to their friends.

I had subsequently a long conversation with the abbot, who was most kind and hospitable. He said the monks had their own ritual, and so far as I could see Howlick is an independent community. In the monastery were many shrines, at each of which was a regular sale of sticks, beads, etc., in which a roaring trade was being done by the monks. In the lower reception room was a number of women, who purchased prayers written by a monk while they waited. For each prayer they paid from sixty cents to a dollar.

The difference in the level of the West River in the wet and dry seasons is about forty feet in its narrow parts. As the waters recede a considerable amount of land is left on the banks available for cultivation and enriched by the deposit from the heavily laden flood waters. These river borders are not allowed to lie idle, for as the river recedes they are carefully cultivated, and crops of vegetables and mulberry leaves taken off before the next rising of the waters. The river banks are then a scene of great activity. In the district about Kumchuk, in which sericulture is a considerable industry, the banks of the river are all planted with mulberry, which ratoons annually and bears three crops of leaves, at each stripping six or seven leaves being left at the top. The worms are fed at first on finely shredded leaves, which have to be changed at least twice daily, the minute young worms being removed to the fresh leaves with the end of a feather. The worms begin to spin in thirty-seven days and continue spinning for seven days. Along the river are many apparently wealthy towns, some showing by a perfect forest of poles like masts with inverted pyramids near the top that a large number of the inhabitants had successfully passed the examinations and received degrees, which entitled them to raise these poles as an honorific distinction before their houses. All mandarins have two such poles erected in front of their yamens.

The West River is at present the principal approach to the province of Yunnan, from which province and from the western portions of Kwangsi a large cattle trade is water-borne to Canton and Hong Kong. From time to time these supplies are intercepted by the river pirates, who sometimes meet their deserts. On one occasion the inhabitants of a certain town, incensed at the murder of one of their people, turned out *en masse* and followed the piratical boat down the river, firing upon her until every one of the robber gang was killed.

CHAPTER IV

The West River sinks into insignificance when compared with the Yangtze, the great river over which is carried the greater portion of the commerce of China. From Wusung, the port of Shanghai, to Hankow — six hundred miles inland — battleships can be navigated, and some direct foreign trade is carried on by the cities upon its banks, though Shanghai is the great centre of foreign trade for all the Yangtze region. The history of the Yangtze is given annually by that most complete and interesting epitome of statistical knowledge — the returns of trade and trade reports by the various Commissioners of the Imperial Maritime Customs. Here everything is dealt with that bears upon the general condition of the country, and one can read at a glance the causes of fluctuations in supply, demand, and prices. In one report we read that production was interfered with by rebellion following a drought. The insurgents, to the number of ten thousand, had armed themselves with hollowed trees for guns, and jingals as well as swords and spears. In the first encounters the insurgents got the better of the Government "troops," who were probably of the ancient type, but on the appearance of two thousand foreign drilled troops they were dispersed. The hollowed trees that did duty for guns was a device not uncommon in old China. The same substitute for cast-iron was tried by the Philippine insurgents in the uprising against Spain; but they had taken the precaution of adding iron rings. They had also large numbers of wooden imitations of Snider rifles, beautifully made, that must have looked formidable, so long as no pretence was made to shoot. The jingal is still in common use in remote districts in China, and was used against our troops in the slight engagements that took place when, under agreement with the Imperial Chinese Government, we proceeded to take over the leased territory of Kowloon. It is a matchlock, the barrel being ten feet long and the bore one inch. In the event of the spherical ball finding its billet, the wound would be of no light matter; but the chances in favour of the target are many, for the jingal requires three men for its manipulation, two of whom act as supports for the barrel, which rests on their shoulders, while the third primes the pan and manipulates the match. When the gun is fired, and the crew of three recover from the shock, it is carried to the rear for reloading, an operation that cannot be performed in a hurry. In the event of a rapid retreat the jingal remains to become the spoil of the captor. At short range, and used against a crowd, a number of jingals would probably be effective, and would present a formidable appearance; but the heroic days of short ranges, waving flags, cheering masses, and flashing steel have passed, and the trained soldier of to-day looks to his sights and to his cover.

If one could follow the ramifications of our trade through the coast ports and rivers and creeks of China, the various products of cotton and velvets, woollen goods, copper, iron, tinned plates, cement, dyes, machinery, oil, railway materials, pepper, sugar, and tea dust, with a host of other things, what an

CHAPTER IV

immense mass of useful and interesting information one would acquire. From the ship to the junk, from the junk to the boat, from the boat to the wheelbarrow, or the mule, and, lastly, to the toiling coolie, who alone can negotiate the dizzy paths of the more remote villages, or the frail means of transport over the raging torrents of the mountain districts. I have said that seaweed is almost unknown on the Chinese coast, and, curiously enough, seaweed is imported in considerable quantities, being used as a food, as in Ireland. The rock seaweed (called dillisk) and carrageen moss are used. For these imports are exchanged a long list of commodities, including eggs, hides (cow and buffalo), skins of all animals (from ass to weazel), silk, tea, tobacco, wood, sesamum, and opium, the latter, mainly from the provinces of Shensi, Szechwan, and Yunnan, being among the most important of the exports. I find on looking over the annual returns of trade for the Yangtze ports for 1906, that the imports of opium for the year amounted to sixty-two thousand one hundred and sixty-one piculs, while the quantity exported amounted to six hundred and forty-three thousand three hundred and seventy-seven piculs. It would be interesting to know if the arrangement entered into by the British Government, that the export of opium from India shall diminish by one-tenth annually until it has ceased, is reciprocal, in so far that not alone shall the exports of the drug from China be diminished in the same proportion, but the area under poppy cultivation be similarly controlled. If no such arrangement has been made, China will have once more demonstrated her astuteness in dealing with unconsidered outbursts of European sentiment. The statements made from time to time by anti-opium enthusiasts have been made in all sincerity, and generally with a desire to approach accuracy as nearly as possible; but, nevertheless, they are merely general statements, made under no authority of reliable statistics, and not seldom unconsciously coloured by an intense desire to emphasize an evil that they consider it impossible to exaggerate. But while it would be extremely difficult to examine systematically into the actual state of opium consumption and its effects upon the population as regards moral degradation and physical deterioration in any Chinese district, these inquiries have been made and reliable statistics obtained in Hong Kong and Singapore, and calculations based on the known consumption of opium in China have been made by competent persons, the result being to show that the statements so loosely made as to the destructive effects of opium-smoking in moderation are not borne out on close examination. My own observation of the Chinese in Hong Kong — a practically Chinese city where every man was free to smoke as much opium as he could afford to purchase — tallies with the conclusion of the exhaustive inquiries since undertaken by order of the home Government. The mass of the Chinese population are very poor, and can support themselves and their families only by incessant labour. When the day's work is done, the coolie who indulges in opium — a very small percentage of the whole — goes to an opium shop, where, purchasing a small quantity of the drug, he retires to a bench or couch, sometimes alone, sometimes with a friend, in which case they lie down on either side of a small lamp and proceed to enjoy their smoke, chatting the while. The pipe is a peculiar shape, looking like an apple with a small hole scooped in it, and stuck on the mouth orifice of a flute. Taking with a long pin looking like a knitting-needle a small quantity (about the size of a pea) of the viscous-prepared opium from the box in which it is sold, the smoker roasts it over the flame of the small lamp until it is of a consistency fit to be placed in the bowl of the pipe, on the outer portion of which the pellet has been kneaded during the heating process. Then placing the bowl to the flame, two or three deep whiffs are taken and swallowed, which exhausts the pellet, when the bowl is cleared out and the process repeated until a state of dreamy slumber or complete torpor is reached, on awaking from which the smoker leaves the place.

When one remembers the exhausting nature of coolies' work in a seaport town it is clear that if opium were smoked to excess the results would be apparent in opium-sodden loafers and beggars; but the contrary is the case, for in no town on earth is the population more efficient and industrious.

A valuable report has lately been issued by the Commission appointed by the governor, to whom the following questions were referred.

- (1) The extent to which excessive indulgence in the smoking of opium prevails in the Straits Settlements.
- (2) Whether the smoking of opium
    - (a) in moderation
    - (b) in excess

has increased in the said Settlements.

- (3) The steps that should be taken ... to eradicate the evils arising from the smoking of opium in the said Settlements.

The Commission included a bishop, three members of the Legislative Council, including the Chinese member, and three independent gentlemen. They examined seventy-five witnesses, including every class in the population, twenty-one of whom were nominated by the anti-opium societies, and presented a report of three hundred and forty-three paragraphs, from which I cull the following excerpts.

Par. 76. We are firmly convinced that the main reason for taking to the habit of smoking opium is the expression among the Chinese of the universal tendency of human nature to some form of indulgence.

Par. 77. The lack of home comforts, the strenuousness of their labour, the severance from family association, and the absence of any form of healthy relaxation in the case of the working classes in Malaya, predispose them to a form of indulgence which, both from its sedative effects and in the restful position in which it must be practised, appeals most strongly to the Chinese temperament.

Par. 91. In the course of the inquiry it has transpired that life insurance companies with considerable experience of the insurance of Chinese lives are willing, *ceteris paribus*, to accept as first-class risks Chinese who smoke two chees (116 grains) of chandu a day, an amount that is by no means within the range of light smoking, and we are informed that these insurance companies are justified in taking these risks. It appears therefore that, in the view of those remarkably well qualified to judge, the opium habit has little or no effect on the duration of life, and there is no evidence before us which would justify our acceptance of the contrary view.

Par. 96. We consider that the tendency of the evidence supports us in the opinion we have formed, as the result of our investigations, that the evils arising from the use of opium are usually the subject of exaggeration. In the course of the evidence it has been pointed out to us that it is difficult even for a medical man to detect the moderate smoker, and it is improbable that the moderate smoker would obtrude himself upon the attention of philanthropists on whose notice bad cases thrust themselves. The tendency of philanthropists to give undue prominence to such bad cases, and to generalize from the observation of them, is undoubtedly a great factor in attributing to the use of opium more widely extended evils than really exist.

Par. 106. The paralysis of the will that is alleged to result from opium-smoking we do not regard as proved, many smokers of considerable quantities are successful in business, and there is no proof that smokers cannot fill positions of considerable responsibility with credit and reliability.

Referring to statements made that the dose must inevitably be constantly increased, the report observes as follows in

Par. 112. We have, further, evidence given in many concrete cases that the dose has not been increased during considerable periods, and we have the remarkable absence of pauperism that should be strikingly prevalent if the theories mentioned above were reasonably applicable to local indulgence in opium.

On the question of enforcing prohibitive legislation, the report observes in

> Par. 133. The poppy is at present cultivated in India, China, Turkey, and Persia, and it may, we consider, be assumed that short of universal suppression of the cultivation effectively carried out, prohibition in one would lead to extended cultivation in others.

The report goes on to deal with the substitution of morphia for opium as demanding the gravest consideration, its effects being infinitely more deleterious than the smoking of opium.

It will be interesting to see how the International Commission that has recently met at Shanghai has dealt with the question. The Imperial Chinese Government has issued drastic regulations, and an Imperial edict has decreed that the growing of the poppy and the smoking of opium shall cease; but the people of China have a way of regarding Imperial edicts that clash with their customs as pious aspirations. If it succeeds, it will have effected a change more complete than any that has taken place since the adoption of the shaved head and the queue at the command of the Manchu conquerors.

The proportion of the volume of trade under the various foreign flags shows of late years a considerable diminution of our trade and an increase of that carried in German bottoms; but this difference in the supply of commodities, while it shows a loss to our shipping, is more apparent than real as regards the commodities themselves. For the last half century or more a large quantity of cotton and other goods ordered through British houses was procured in Germany and shipped from English ports. But with the passing of the Merchandise Marks Act, a change was soon observed. When the astute Chinese trader saw printed upon his cotton cloth the advertisement that it was made in Germany, he asked the German Consul about it, and concluded that it would be better business to order it from the maker direct, which he did. The equally astute German arrived at the conclusion that as this large direct trade had developed it would be well to build the ships to carry it under its own flag, and save the transport and turnover in England. The result was a great increase of German shipping to the East, and with the increase of German argosies came the proposal, as a natural sequence, that a German navy should be created to ensure their protection. Thus the Act that was hailed with such appreciation became the greatest and most valuable advertisement ever given by one nation to another, and German technical knowledge, thoroughness, and business capacity have taken full advantage of the situation. Ten years ago the German flag in Hong Kong harbour was comparatively infrequent. To-day the steamers of Germany frequently outnumber our own in that great port.

The life of town and country is more sharply divided in China than in Europe, for the absence of local protection drives all wealthy men to the security of the walled towns and cities. The aspect of all the great cities south of the Yangtze is pretty much the same, and there is not much difference in the life of the communities. The cities are encircled by walls about twenty-five feet high and from fifteen to twenty feet on top, with square towers at intervals, and great gateways at the four cardinal points. The north gate at Hangchow, at the extremity of the Grand Canal, is the most beautiful that I have seen in China. Eight stone monoliths supported an elaborate structure of three stories narrowing to the summit that was finished by a boat-shaped structure with ornamental ends and a curved roof. Every portion of the great structure of stone was beautifully carved, the upper portions being perforated. The carved work was exquisite, figures standing in bold relief, and flowers and foliage being undercut so that a stick could have been passed behind them. The walls of Nanking and Suchow are each thirty-six miles in circumference, but within the walls are large areas that have probably never been built over. The vacant spaces may always have been used for agricultural purposes, the crops enabling the inhabitants to withstand a siege. Many of the splendid buildings of these old cities have disappeared or are now in ruins, but here and there the tiled roofs, beautiful in their curved design and brilliant glaze of green or yellow enamel, remain to testify to the innate artistic feeling of the Chinese people. The Ming tombs at Nanking, with the mile-long approach through a double row of elephants, camels, chitons, horses, etc., each ten and a half feet high and carved from a single block, are monuments that, unlike the great bronze astronomical instruments that erstwhile adorned the walls of Peking, no conquering host could carry away. On the back of each of the elephants is a heap of stones, every Chinese who passes feeling it a religious duty to wish, generally either for wealth or a son, when he casts up a stone. If it remains, the answer is favourable; if not, he continues his course in sadness, but not without hope. The porcelain tower of Nanking has disappeared, but the bronze summit, fifteen feet in diameter, remains on its site.

Inside the city walls the streets are narrow and sometimes filthy. Smells abound, but Chinese are apparently oblivious to what we consider offensive smells; and from a hygienic point of view it is certain that foul smells are better than sewer-gas, which, though it cannot be characterized as dirt, is decidedly matter in the wrong place.

Peking is unlike any of the southern cities. Its streets are wide, and the mixture of peoples from the north gives variety and colour to the street scenes. Here one meets long strings of laden camels bearing their burdens from Mongolia, and issuing grumbling protests as they follow the bell of their leader. Peking carts with richly ornamented wheels but no springs ply over the raised centre of the broad but filthy streets, the mud of winter and the dust of summer assuaging the jolting of the picturesque but uncomfortable vehicles. Sometimes in the carts are richly apparelled ladies, who are attended by mounted servants. Now and again may be seen immense funeral biers bright with red lacquer and gilding, and resting upon a platform of bamboos large enough to admit from twenty to fifty or sixty bearers. Should the funeral be that of a high official, as many as a hundred bearers are sometimes engaged. This is a form of ostentation impossible in the narrow streets of the southern cities. Peking is really four cities within the immense outer walls, which are fifty feet high and probably thirty or forty feet broad on top. On the portion of the wall commanding the legations some of the hardest fighting of the siege took place. The Temple of Heaven and the Temple of Agriculture are situated to the right and left of the south gate of the outer wall. Each temple stands in a park, and in the one the Emperor on the first day of the Chinese New Year offers a sacrifice on the great white marble terrace, and prays for blessings upon all his people, while in the Temple of Agriculture the Emperor, attended by all the great officials, attends on the first day of spring for the performance of the ceremonies, as laid down by ancient custom. This ceremony in honour of the opening of spring is one of the principal functions of the year. The Emperor, with all the Court, attends at the Temple of Agriculture in state to plough a furrow. The buffalo that draws the plough is decorated with roses and other flowers, and the plough is covered with silk of the Imperial yellow. The ground has been carefully softened, and a hard path arranged on which the Emperor walks while he guides the plough, before doing which he removes his embroidered jacket and tucks up the long silk coat round his waist, as a carpenter does when he wants to get his apron out of the way and leave his legs free. After his Majesty has ploughed his furrow, three princes, each with a buffalo and plough decorated with red silk, plough each three furrows, followed by nine of the principal officials, whose ploughs and buffaloes are decorated like those of the princes. A rice is then sown called the red lotus, which when reaped is presented as an offering — half on the altar at the Temple of Agriculture, half on that before the tablets of the Imperial family in the royal ancestral hall.

This ceremony is of very ancient date, and indicates the high position held by the agriculturist in the estimation of the Chinese. In the books of Chow, written probably about 1000 B.C., in writing against luxurious ease, it is written, "King Wăn dressed meanly, and gave himself to the work of tranquillization and to that of husbandry."

To Peking, as the centre of Chinese official life, flock all the higher mandarins from time to time, each high official — viceroy, governor, or taotai, or lower ranks — to give an account of their stewardship at the expiration of their term of office, and to solicit a renewed appointment. Should a viceroy have acquired, say, three millions of dollars during his three years' term of office, it will be necessary for him to disburse at least one million in presents to various palace officials before he can hope for an audience and for further employment. Many of the officials put their savings into porcelain rather than invest them in speculation, or deposit them in savings banks. Some of this porcelain is buried or concealed in a safe place, and when the owner requires money he disposes of a piece. It is thought in England that great bargains of valuable porcelain can be picked up in any Chinese town. This is a mistake. Of course, great bargains may possibly be picked up anywhere, but good porcelain is highly valued in China as in Europe. Shown a very fine vase by the principal dealer in curiosities of Peking, he quoted the price at seventeen thousand dollars. The result of the Chinese custom of buying porcelain as a savings bank investment, and its re-sale when money is required, is a constant traffic in good porcelain, which can generally be procured, at its full value.

CHAPTER V

The peasant cultivator of China spends a life of intermittent industry. In the north there is but one annual crop, but in the south two crops are grown. The principal cultivation being rice, he is perforce constrained to the system of co-operation, as, there being no fences, all the rice crop of a large flat area, sometimes minutely subdivided, must be reaped at the same time, so that when the crop has been removed the cattle and buffaloes may roam over the flat for what pasturage they can pick up before the flooding of the land and preparation for the next crop.

In the event of any farmer being late with his sowing, he must procure seed of a more rapidly growing kind, some kinds of rice showing a difference of a month or more in the time that elapses from sowing to reaping. But even when the crop is down and growing, no grass that may be found on the edges of the paths or canals is allowed to go to waste. Small children may then be seen seated sideways on the broad backs of the buffaloes while the beasts graze upon the skirting pasture, the children preventing them from injuring the growing crops.

The first crop is sown about April and reaped early in July, the second late in July and reaped at the end of September. After the rice, which has generally been sown very thickly in a nursery, has been transplanted to the flooded fields and taken root, the ground is gone over and the mud heaped with the feet around each plant. The ground is manured when the rice is about a foot high with pig manure, mixed with lime and earth, and scattered by hand at a time when the water is low. If the crop looks poor the manure is carefully applied round each plant, and sometimes if it is still very backward, when the water is around it, the manure is poured over it in a liquid state. The water is kept on the rice field until a very short time before reaping, and after the crop is in full ear the Chinese like to have three days' rain, which they say improves the yield very materially.

When the rice is six or eight inches over the water, which is then about three inches deep, large flocks of ducks and geese may be seen feeding on the frogs, etc., to be found in the paddy fields (paddy is the term for rice before it has been husked), attended by a man or boy, who carries a long bamboo pole with a bunch of bamboo leaves tied at the top. When the evening comes a shake of his pole brings all the flock, sometimes numbering hundreds, out of the field, and as they emerge on the path the last duck or goose receives a whack of the bunch of leaves. It is amusing to see how this is realized by the birds, who waddle along at top speed to avoid being last. Once on the path the herd goes in front, and, placing his pole against the base of a bank, all the flock jump over it, being counted as they go. Ducks are reared in amazing numbers in Southern China, the eggs being hatched in fermenting paddy husks. Every country shop has displayed a number of dried ducks, the fowl being cut in half and spread out under pressure. But as articles of food nothing comes amiss; rats are dried in the same way and sold, though the house rat is not usually eaten, the rat of commerce being the rodent found in the rice fields. Besides rice, the farmer grows crops of rape, fruit, and a large quantity of vegetables. Mulberry trees are the main crop in the silk regions, and in the provinces bordering the Yangtze tea is produced, while to the westward the cultivation of the poppy assumes large proportions. In the economy of the Chinese farmer the pig plays as prominent a part as in Ireland, for the pig is a save-all, to which all scraps are welcome. The Chinese pig is usually black. It has a peculiarly hollow back, the belly almost trailing on the ground, and it fattens easily. A roast sucking-pig is always a *pièce de resistance* at a feast.

The Chinese farmer is thrifty, but he has his distractions in card-playing and gambling in various ways that could only be devised by Chinese ingenuity. He loves a quail fight or a cricket fight, the latter being an amusement that sometimes brings a concourse of thousands together. A large mat-shed is erected and in this is placed the cricket pit. The real arena of the fight is a circular bowl with a flat bottom about seven inches in diameter. Two crickets being placed in it are excited to fury by having their backs tickled by a rat's bristle inserted in the end of a small stick, such as a pen handle. The rival crickets fight with great fury until one turns tail and is beaten. Many thousands of dollars are wagered at times upon these contests, and the most intense excitement prevails. When a man has been fortunate enough to capture a good fighting cricket he feeds it on special meal. Such a known cricket sometimes changes hands for a considerable sum. After all, the value of a cricket, like a race-horse, is what it may be able to win. As the

CHAPTER V

initial expense of a cricket is only the trouble of catching it, this is a form of excitement within reach of the poorest, and the villager may have in gambling for a cash (the tenth part of a cent) as much excitement as the richer town-dweller who wagers in dollars.

The farmer's house is not luxurious in its furniture, but it is sufficient for his wants. With the exception of the table almost everything is made of bamboo, which, with the aid of fire and water, can be bent to any shape, but there is great diversity in the lamp of pottery or pewter or brass, the latter being somewhat similar in shape to the ancient Roman lamp. The bed is simply a flat board, over which a grass or palm leaf mat is laid. The pillow is a half round piece of pottery about ten inches long and four inches high. A common form is that of a figure on hands and knees, the back forming the pillow. The careful housewife places her needlework inside the pillow, which makes an effective workbasket. In winter the pottery pillow is replaced by one of lacquer and leather, which is not so cold. Over his door will be found a beehive, made of a drum of bamboo two feet long by twelve inches in diameter and covered with dried clay, while his implements of husbandry — consisting of a wooden plough of the same shape as may be seen on Egyptian ancient monuments, and which with the harness he carries on his shoulder to the field, a hoe, and a wooden "rake" of plain board to smooth the mud on which the rice will be sown — can be accommodated in the corner. He is not very clean and has a lofty contempt for vermin; but sometimes he will indulge in the luxury of a flea-trap, made of a joint of bamboo three inches in diameter, the sides cut out, leaving only enough wood to preserve the shape. This he carries in his sleeve, but what he inserts as a trap I have not been able to discover.

Apart from his gambling his distractions are a visit to the temple before or after crop time, a marriage, a funeral, a procession, or a pilgrimage to one of the seven holy mountains of China. He has not often more than one wife, who, being entirely at his mercy, rules him with a rod of iron, and to whom as a rule he leaves the emotional part of the religion of the family. To her falls all the anxious care of the children, and horrible fears assail her lest the evil spirits, against whose machinations all the ingenuity of her religious superstitions is exerted, should get possession of any of her boys. To this end she will dress the boys as girls, and indulge in make-believes that would not puzzle the silliest devil that ever tormented a Chinese mother. Nor does she neglect religious duties, for she will be seen in the temple praying devoutly, and then taking up the two kidney-shaped pieces of wood, flat on one side and round on the other, that are found on the altar before the god, she will place the flat sides together between her palms and flinging them up observe the position in which they fall. If both flat sides come up, it is good; if the round, then it is evil; if one of each, there is no answer. This she repeats three times; or going to a bamboo in which are a number of canes, each bearing a number, she shakes it, as Nestor shook the helmet of Agamemnon, until one falls out, when she looks for the corresponding number among a quantity of yellow sheets of paper hung upon the wall where she reads the mystic answer to her prayer.

It is not easy for the casual inquirer to understand the religious beliefs of the Chinese. In many ways intensely materialistic, the people have a living faith, at least in reincarnation or recurring life; and while their spiritual attitude is rather a fear of evil demons than a belief in a merciful God, yet there is among them a spirit of reverence and of thankfulness for favours received. One day at Chekwan Temple — a very fine and richly ornamented temple on the Pearl River — I saw a fisherman and his family enter with a basket of fish and some fruits, which he laid upon the altar. Then, first striking the drum to call the attention of the god, the family prayed devoutly, while the father poured a libation seven times upon the altar. I asked the priest what it meant, and he answered that the man had had a good take of fish the previous night and was returning thanks. Sometimes when a member of the family is ill they will go to the temple and have a prayer written, then burning the paper, they take home the ashes, and administer them as a medicine. Again, in a temple in Canton one pillar is covered with paper figures of men, which are tied to the pillar upside down. Asking the meaning I was told that these were tied on by the light-o'-loves of young Chinese who, having taken a wife, had put an end to the temporary arrangements as common in a Chinese city as in the centres of Western civilization. The abandoned ones vainly hoped that by timely incantations and tying on of the figures their protectors might be induced to return to them. But the great annual excitement to the peasant under normal conditions is the theatrical performance that takes place in every district. The company brings its own theatre, an enormous mat-shed erection capable of accommodating an audience of a thousand people.

CHINA

This is erected in a few days, and for a week or more historical or social plays are performed. The actors make up and dress upon the stage, on which the more prominent members of the audience are sometimes accommodated. All the actors are men, as women are not allowed to perform; but the men who take women's parts could not be distinguished from females, and some are very highly paid. The dresses are very gorgeous. In historical plays all the actors wear long beards and moustaches which completely cover the mouth. The bad character of the play is always distinguished by having the face darkened and with a white patch on the nose. The play is in the form of an opera in which the singers intone their parts in a simple recurring time, being accompanied in unison by a couple of stringed instruments of curious form; but when an important entry is made or one of the oft-recurring combats take place, large cymbals clash with deafening noise. This is never done while the singing dialogue is proceeding. The properties are in a large box on the stage. If an actor is going over a bridge the attendants, who are moving about, place a table with a chair at either side, put over it a cloth, and the bridge is complete. The actor walks over and the table is removed. Should he mount a horse, or get into a chair, conventional movements convey the fact to the audience. In the combats one man is always slain. Then the attendant walks forward and drops a roll of white paper or cloth before him, when the slain man gets up and walks out. In Japan matters are somewhat differently done. There are always two attendants in black with wide flowing sleeves, who are supposed to be invisible. When a character is slain one stands in front, spreads his arms, and

CHAPTER V

the defunct walks off, the invisible attendant moving after him, keeping between him and the audience.

In social plays the actors are no longer in gorgeous historic costumes, but are clad in modern dress. When a very poor man came on he indicated his poverty by making the movements of cracking vermin on his clothes between his nails.

It is singular how little one misses the scenery, and the audience takes the keenest interest in the plays, sometimes being moved to tears at the tragic parts.

The position of the actor is very low in the Chinese scale, no actor or child of an actor being permitted to present himself for public examination; the brotherhood of the sock and buskin is a very large community.

When the play is finished, if there are wealthy men present servants come in laden with strings of copper cash, which are laid upon the stage.

But these are the incidents of country life in normal times. When rains are short and rivers run low, and the rice crop fails, then gaunt famine stalks over the arid land, and discontent and misery are apt to lead to grave local troubles, the people looking upon such a visitation as a direct intimation that the Emperor, as represented by the local officials, had incurred the displeasure of heaven and lost the confidence of the gods. This feeling makes for rebellion, and rebellion in China, when it is faced by Government, is dealt with in a manner so ruthless as to make one shudder.

In 1903 a famine with the usual concomitants developed in the province of Kwangsi, and harrowing descriptions of the condition of affairs came to Hong Kong, where a relief committee was formed at once. An official was sent up on behalf of the committee to inquire and report, and on his return he gave an account of what he had seen. A troublesome rebellion had broken out, and in the course of its suppression many prisoners had been taken. These wretches, with large numbers of criminals, were being executed, a general gaol delivery being thus effected, the magistrate holding that as there was not enough food for honest people none could be spared for criminals. The starving population had been reduced to such extremity that they were eating the bodies. At the same time the authorities and the gentry were doing everything in their power to relieve the suffering of the people; but all were miserably poor, and no taxes were being collected. The Hong Kong Relief Committee's representative, who had taken a first consignment of rice with him, was offered every facility by the magistrate, who not alone gave him a guard, but sent a launch to tow the rice junk up the river, sending a guard with it. The state of brutality to which the community had been reduced was shown by the following occurrence related to the representative by one of his guards, who told the story with an evident feeling that the incident redounded to the credit of the "party of order." A short time before, information having reached the local authority of the whereabouts of a "robber family," a party, including the narrator, went to the village and seized the entire family. The man they cut open, took out the entrails, cooked and ate them in the presence of the dying wretch. They cut the breasts off the woman, cooked and ate them in the same way. The woman he described as sobbing during the operation. The two were then killed. As the "soldiers" did not care to kill the children themselves, they handed knives to a number of surrounding children, who hacked the little ones to death.

This is a lurid story, but the sequel shows that even in China danger lurks in too ferocious exercise of despotic power, however well intended. The magistrate was unceasing in his efforts to cope with the famine, with the added troubles of a rebellion, in fighting which the advantage was not always with his troops. Rice was being poured into the famine districts by committees established in Hong Kong and Canton, and every assistance that could be given was afforded to them by the magistrate, who was an educated gentleman and apparently full of pity for the famishing people. His unvarying civility to the working members of the Hong Kong committee who were engaged in the distribution was at the close of their proceedings duly and gratefully acknowledged; but the warm thanks of the committee never reached him. A new viceroy had been appointed to Canton, who, on proceeding to the famine district to make personal inquiry, found that the magistrate had not been just, but had executed as criminals innocent people, among them being a secret agent sent up by the viceroy in advance to inquire into the real state of affairs. On finding this he degraded the magistrate, who thereupon committed suicide. When one reads of the reckless ferocity with which life was taken it is astonishing that he was not put an end to by poison long before the interference of the viceroy; for poisoning is not unknown, the plant named in China muk-tong being used. It is inodorous and tasteless, but if boiled in water used for tea it is almost certain death.

CHINA

The life of the coast cities where East meets West is full of interest. Every treaty port has its foreign concession, where the consuls reign supreme, and a Western system of police and municipal arrangements is adopted. Tientsin, Shanghai, Ningpo, Fuchow, Amoy, and Canton, as well as the Yangtze ports, all have on their borders large areas over which the Chinese Government has abandoned its territorial rights, and all offences or disputes are dealt with in European magistrates' or consular courts with the exception of Shanghai, where for certain offences the cases are tried in a mixed court, under the jurisdiction of a Chinese and a European magistrate. The sudden contrast from the foreign concession at Shanghai to the Chinese city is most striking; on the one side a splendid bund along the river bank, well kept public gardens, an excellent police force (mounted and foot), broad streets in which are fine shops displaying the newest European patterns, well appointed gharries standing on their appointed ranks for hire at moderate fares, and for the poorer Chinese the ubiquitous Chinese wheelbarrow — mentioned by Milton — that is palpably the one-wheeled progenitor of the Irish jaunting-car. The axle of the barrow is in the centre, the large wheel working in a high well on either side of which are two seats. There is no weight on the handles when the legs are lifted; the barrow coolie has therefore only to preserve the balance and push. These barrows are used everywhere in the Yangtze region, and are suitable for carrying heavy loads over interior tracks too narrow for two wheels. In Shanghai they are not alone used for transport of heavy burdens, but form the usual means of locomotion for the Chinese of the

CHAPTER V

labouring class who prefer the luxury of driving to walking. In the morning, as in the evening, when going to work or coming from it, as many as six people may be seen sitting three a side and being pushed along by one coolie with apparent ease, or now and again one or two men on one side are balanced by a large pig tied on the other.

Along the river front, where the bund is prolonged into Chinese territory, the Western influence is seen in the police arrangements, Chinese police, or "lukongs," being similarly attired as their Chinese brethren in the "Settlements." But inside the walls the scene changes, and the Chinese city is found, simple but not pure, as Shanghai city is among the very dirtiest in all China. Yet it has its picturesque and somewhat imposing spots near the great temples. Outside the city bounds is the usual burial-place, on the border of the flat plain that surrounds Shanghai. Here the custom is to deposit the coffins on the ground, the tombs being sometimes built of brick, or the coffin being covered with thatch, while in some cases the coffins are simply left upon the ground without any covering. It must be explained that the Chinese coffin is a peculiarly solid case, built in a peculiar manner with very thick slabs of wood In every direction are peach orchards, which when in blossom present as beautiful a sight as the famed cherry blossom of Japan. All around the plain is intersected with deep drains, the muddy bottoms of which the sporting members of the Shanghai Hunt Club now and again make involuntary acquaintance. The position of Shanghai, situated as it is near the mouth of the Yangtze, marks it out as the future emporium of the commerce of Central China, through which must ebb and flow the ever-growing trade of nine of the eighteen provinces of the Middle Kingdom. The social intercourse between the foreign and the Chinese communities is very restricted, a restriction that cannot be laid entirely at the door of either side; but until the division becomes less clearly and sharply marked there can be no well grounded prospect of such community of feeling as will make trade relations comfortable, when the now blinking eyes of the sleeping giant have fully opened and he realizes his strength and power to command attention to his demand for reciprocal rights among the great nations of the earth.

To a foreigner the most impressive city in China is Canton, with its teeming population and intense activity. The foreign settlement of Shameen lies along the bank of the Pearl River, and on the land side is surrounded by a canal, the only entrance to the settlement being over two carefully guarded bridges. Here everything is purely Western — Western architecture, Western lawns, Western games; the flags of all the foreign nations fly over their respective consulates; and but for the Chinese domestics that one sees here and there, one might, if he turned his gaze from the river, with its maze of junks and boats of every kind, forget that he was not walking in the wealthy residential suburb of a European town. But once over the bridge and past the solid rows of stores — once the godowns of the European hongs — every trace of European influence is gone, and we enter through the city walls into a scene such as has existed in Chinese cities for centuries. The streets vary in width from six to ten feet, and are all flagged with granite slabs, and in these narrow streets is a dense mass of blue-robed Chinese, all intent upon business except when a foreigner enters into a shop to make a purchase, which always attracts a curious and observing crowd. Narrow as are the streets, the effect is still more contracted by the hanging sign-boards, painted in brilliant colours and sometimes gilt letters, that hang outside each shop. These signboards are sometimes ten to twelve feet long, and each trade has its own particular colouring and shape. The effect of the sign-boards, the colour of the open shops, and the gay lanterns that hang at almost every door, is very fine, and gives an idea of wealth and artistic sentiment. Every shop removes its shutters in the morning, and as there are usually no windows, the effect is that of moving through an immense bazaar, in which every known trade is being carried on, while the wares are being sold at an adjoining counter. In one shop will be found the most expensive silks and other stuffs, or rather in a row of shops, for each particular business affects certain parts of the street. Thus at one end may be a succession of shops with the most delicate and beautiful commodities, while the continuation is devoted to butchers' stalls, or fishmongers', the sudden transition being proclaimed to every sense, and outraging our feeling of the fitness of things. In the shops will be seen men at work upon the beautiful fans for which Canton is famed; in another the shoemaker or the hatter ply their more homely trade. Tailors, stocking-makers, carpenters, blacksmiths, all are diligently at work, while here and there, poring carefully over a piece of jewellery or brass or silver work, may be seen the feather-worker attaching the delicate patterns made with the brilliant feathers of the kingfisher, the work being so minute that young men and boys only can do it, and so trying that their eyesight can only stand it for about two years. At the corners of the streets are seen teahouses, the entire front being elaborately carved from ground to roof and glittering with brilliant gilding. Ivory-cutters carry on their trade, and jade and porcelain are displayed. A great feature in many of the streets is the bird shops, filled with singing birds or birds of brilliant plumage, of which the Chinese are very fond, wealthy Chinese gentlemen giving sometimes large sums for ivory cages for their favourites. In places the streets are covered for short distances. These gay shops are not usually found in the side streets, where the rougher trades — the butcher, the fishmonger, and the greengrocer — predominate. In these particular streets the smells are to European sense simply abominable, but appreciation or otherwise of smells is possibly a racial as well as an individual peculiarity. Among us musk is the delight of some and the horror of others.

Although too narrow for wheeled traffic, the noise of the streets is considerable, as coolies, carrying great baskets of goods or perhaps vegetables, shout panting warnings to the crowd, and all must make way for the laden coolie. Now and again a mandarin rides past, attended by his servants, or is carried in his official chair, when everybody makes way for him with the most surprising alacrity. It is easy to see that the people recognize the all but despotic power that always notes the officials of a practically democratic community. The general idea that strikes a stranger when going for the first time through these narrow streets with their dense crowds is one of awe, feeling as if enmeshed in the labyrinths of a human ant-hill, from which there could be no hope of escape if the crowd made any hostile movement. But the interests of Canton are not exhausted in her crowded streets, with the marvellous absence of any jostling — the chair coolies never touching anybody with their chairs, even though they fill up half the width of the streets — for there are the various temples that have been described *ad nauseam*; the water clock that has been going for over six centuries; the mint, where the Government produces from time to time coins of not always clearly determined fineness; and the City of the Dead, where for a moderate payment an apartment may be engaged, in which a deceased member of a family can be accommodated until such time as the geomancer can find an auspicious position for the grave. Some of these apartments, which are all kept admirably clean, have tables on which are left the pipe of the inmate, while paper figures stand by to hand him, if necessary, the spiritual aroma of his favourite food when alive.

The guild-houses of Canton are well built and richly ornamented structures. These guild-houses are the club-houses of various provinces, or the local club of the members of different trades. Even the beggars have their guild in Canton, where strange members of that ancient and honourable profession may obtain accommodation, and permission to ply their occupation as mendicants on payment of a fee. Every beggar so licensed carries a badge, bearing which he has the right to enter a shop and demand alms. Among the procession of mandarins with their brilliant entourage who assembled to meet Liu Kun Yi, the viceroy at Nanking, on his return from Peking, in 1900, was the mandarin head of the beggars. He was arrayed in the correct and rich robes of his rank, and had his place in the procession exactly as the other mandarins, who were each surrounded or followed by their staff and their troops. The mandarin of the beggars' guild was carried in his official chair, and around him and following him was the most extraordinary and motley crowd of beggars, all in their workaday rags and tatters. Had they but arms of any sort they might have given points to Falstaff's ragged regiment. Every shopkeeper is visited at least once daily by a member of the fraternity, and whether by law or by custom he must contribute some small amount. The system is possibly a form of outdoor relief, and if one but knew its inner working it would probably be found to be a fairly satisfactory solution of a difficulty that is exercising the wits of anxious social investigators in England.

If the shopkeeper refuses to submit to the customary demand he may find a beggar, afflicted with some loathsome disease, seated at the door of his shop, where he will remain until the honour of the guild has been satisfied by a suitable donation, for there will be no stern policeman to order the persistent beggar to move on. One of the most painful sights that I have ever seen was a collection of lepers who had been allowed to take possession of a small dry patch in the middle of a deep swamp in the new territory of Kowloon. The only entrance was by a narrow path roughly raised over the swamp level. Here they had constructed huts from pieces of boxes, through which the rain entered freely. Each morning the miserable creatures dragged themselves to the neighbouring villages, the inhabitants of which charitably placed rice for them before their

CHAPTER V

doors. I have never seen a more miserable collection of human beings. I had proper huts erected for them on neighbouring high ground, where at least they were free from the danger of being flooded out, and had shelter from rain and wind. There is a regular leper hospital in Canton.

It must not be assumed that Canton is entirely a town of retail shops, for there are many important factories there, some of the houses of business covering large areas, where hundreds of men are employed in the various manufactures. Crowded as is the business part of the city, one wonders that it is not devastated by fire; but over every shop vessels of water are kept upon the roof, ready for instant service. The value of land is very great, the average value being fourteen dollars a square foot, which is roughly about sixty thousand pounds per acre. But the narrow streets of Canton can be very imposing when a high foreign official is paying a visit of ceremony to the viceroy. On one side of the street is a continuous line of soldiers — the streets are too narrow for a double line — each company with its banner, while the other side is occupied by a dense crowd that fills the shops and stands silently to see the procession of official chairs go by. The streets are not alone swept, but carefully washed, so that they are perfectly clean. At each ward-gate is stationed half a dozen men with long trumpets, like those upon which Fra Angelico's angels blew their notes of praise, and from these trumpets two long notes are sounded — one high, the other low. In the courtyard of the viceroy's yamen is stationed a special guard of about one hundred and fifty men, richly dressed and carrying such arms as one sees in very old Chinese pictures —

great curved blades on long poles, tridents, etc. — while thirty or forty men stand with banners of purple, yellow, blue, or red silk, each some twelve feet square, mounted on poles at least twenty feet long. The effect is singularly picturesque. The viceroy's yamen is situated more than a mile from the river, so that a large number of troops are required to line the streets. The yamen is surrounded by an extensive park, in which is some good timber. Another fine park surrounds the building once occupied by the British Consul, but now used by the cadets of the Straits Settlements and Hong Kong, who on appointment to the Colonies are sent for two years to Canton, there to study Chinese.

However busy the high official in China may be, his daily life is passed in quiet, if not in peace. With him there are no distracting sounds of street traffic, no hoot of motor-cars, no roar and rumble of motor-omnibuses, no earthquake tremors from heavy cart traffic. The streets are too narrow for this, and the yamen and the office are separated from any possible interference with business by street noises. The business of the yamen is, however, rarely done in solitude, for the yamen "runners," as the crowd of lictors and messengers are called, overrun the entire place, and the most important conversations are carried on in the presence of pipe-bearers and other personal attendants, to say nothing of curious outsiders, that almost precludes the possibility of inviolable secrecy. It is possible that where foreigners are not mixed up in the matter there may not be so many anxious listeners, but there are few things about a yamen that are not known by those whose interest it is to know them.

CHAPTER V

The official proceeds with his work upon lines that have been deeply grooved by custom, and however energetic he may be, he is careful not to make violent changes, nor will he hastily leave the beaten track. As a rule, no community becomes violently agitated by inaction on the part of a government or of an official, however much it may be deprecated. In China the only fear in such a case would be from the action of the censors, who are appointed in various parts of the empire, and who have proved by their denunciation of even the highest officials for sins of omission, as well as commission, that China possesses among her officials men whose fearlessness and independence are equal to that of men of other races, whose honoured names have come down to us in song and story.

The rigid etiquette of China preserves a dignity in the conduct of all public business, and it is against the first principles of an educated Chinaman to use rough or harsh terms that would be considered vulgar. The written language is so capable of different interpretations that in treaties with China, which are generally written in three languages — Chinese, French or English — and the language of the contracting countries, it is always stipulated that in construing the terms of the treaty one of the two languages, not the Chinese, is to be taken as interpreting its true meaning. This does not necessarily infer dishonest intentions on the part of the Chinese; but the fact is that as each one of the many thousands of Chinese characters may mean more than one thing, the real meaning has sometimes to be inferred from the context, so that there are peculiar difficulties attending the close and accurate interpretation of a treaty or dispatch. It is popularly supposed that Sir Robert Hart and Sir J. McLeavy Brown are the only foreigners who have complete mastery of the art of writing Chinese so as to ensure the accurate expression of the meaning to be conveyed. The yamen of a high official, with his residence, covers a large area, as no house is built more than one story high. Such a building might by its dominating height interfere disastrously with the *fung sui* of even a city, and is always bitterly resented. The steeples of churches have something to answer for in this way in keeping alive the spirit of antagonism fostered by the daily maledictions of the Chinese, who bear patiently with submission rather than acquiescence the presence of a dominant foreign influence that, if they have any living superstition on the subject, must convey to them an impression of evil. The yamen usually consists of a series of courtyards, off which are built the apartments for the numerous staff as well as the private apartments of the family, and in one of these, when the business of the day is concluded, the official receives the visits of his friends and smokes the calumet of peace, or plays one of those complicated games of Chinese chess to whose intricate rules and moves our game of chess is simplicity itself. Sometimes after his work he indulges in his pipe of opium, after the manner of our own three-bottle men of the last century. The late Liu Kun Yi, the able Viceroy of Nanking, who with Chang Chi Tung, his neighbouring viceroy, kept the Yangtze provinces quiet through the Boxer troubles was a confirmed opium-smoker. But one thing he never does — he never hurries. Haste is to him undignified, and he eschews it. In his official dealings he will adopt methods that would not pass muster in our courts; but from the Emperor to the coolie those methods are understood and accepted. Much might be written on the ethics of what we call official corruption; but let the facts be what they may, the people understand the system, the Government understand it, and there is no popular demonstration against it. Nor must we forget that official "irregularity" is not unknown outside China.

The social side of the life of a Chinese mandarin is not confined to his own yamen. He is fond of visiting his friends and engaging in intellectual conversation over a friendly cup of tea — and such tea! We have no idea in Europe of the exquisite delicacy of the best Chinese tea as prepared by a Chinese host. The tea is made by himself, the leaves being only allowed to remain in the freshly boiled water for four or five minutes. It is then poured into cups of delicate porcelain, about the size of a liqueur glass, and sipped without the addition of milk or sugar. After the tea has been drunk, the aroma of the cup is enjoyed. The perfume is delicious.

CHAPTER VI

The houses of the wealthy inhabitants are on the east side of the city, and are separated from the streets by high walls. On entering the grounds, the visitor passes through several courtyards and reception halls, supported on beautifully carved granite pillars, a wealthy Chinese gentleman sparing no expense in the lavish and tasteful decoration of his home. From the courtyards one enters the gardens, in which there is invariably a pond in which water-flowers — lilies, lotus, etc. — are grown, and in which there are shoals of goldfish. A rockery is generally added, with quaintly contrived approaches and caverns, and a bridge over the pond leads now and again to a small island on which a decorated tea-house has been erected. The bridge is always angular, like those that are seen on the old blue china plates. In one large house, from which the owner was absent, were some specimens of hammered iron-work that were the very perfection of artistic workmanship. They were blades of grass, reeds, and flowers, each specimen being placed in a window between two panes of glass. These specimens of iron-work were made about four hundred and fifty years ago by an artist whose name is still held in honour. Large sums have been offered for them, but the fortunate owner holds them more precious than gold.

A great feature of Canton is its flower-boats, of which many hundreds are moored together, and form regular streets. These boats are all restaurants, and here the wealthy young Chinamen entertain each other at their sumptuous feasts. The giver of the entertainment always engages four or five young women for each guest, who sit behind the gentlemen and assist in their entertainment. As the feast is a long function, consisting of many courses, it is not necessary for the guests to be present during the entire function. Sometimes a guest will put in an appearance for one or two courses. Music is played and songs are sung, and possibly there may be ramifications of the entertainment into which one does not pry too closely; but again there are regulated customs in China openly acknowledged and less harmful than the ignored but no less existing canker that has eaten into the heart of Western civilization.

The wives and daughters of officials are in small towns at a certain disadvantage, for etiquette demands that they shall confine their visits to their social equals, who are not many. In large cities they have the ladies of the wealthy merchants to visit, and they are by no means devoid of subjects of conversation. They take a keen interest in public affairs, and exercise no small an amount of influence upon current topics. Many of the Chinese ladies are well educated, and have no hesitation in declaring their views on matters connected with their well-being. A very short time ago there was in Canton a public meeting of women to protest against an unpopular measure. One result of missionary effort in China has been the education of a large number of Chinese women of different classes in English, which many Chinese ladies speak fluently. When Kang

Yu Wei, the Chinese reformer, was in Hong Kong, having taken refuge there after his flight from Peking, his daughter was a young Chinese lady who spoke only her own language. Two years later, during which time the family had resided in the Straits Settlements, this lady passed through Hong Kong, speaking English fluently. She was on her way to the United States to pursue her studies.

The movement for reform that has begun to agitate China is by no means confined to the men. In 1900 a women's conference met in Shanghai, under the presidency of Lady Blake, to consider the question of the home life of the women of China. The conference sat for four days, during which papers were read by both European and Chinese ladies on various social questions and customs affecting all classes of the women of China. The conference covered a wide range of subjects: — Treatment of Children; Daughters-in-law; Betrothal of Young Children and Infants; Girl Slavery in China; Foot-binding; Marriage Customs; Funeral Customs; Social Customs; and its proceedings contain valuable accounts at first hand of the conditions and customs of women from every part of the Middle Kingdom. The following remarks were made by the president at the conclusion of the conference.

"We have now concluded the consideration of the subjects that were selected for discussion at this conference on the 'Home Life of Chinese Women.' We have all, I am sure, been keenly interested in the excellent papers and addresses with which we have been favoured, containing so much information from all parts of this vast empire that must have been new to many of us. I regret to find that the lot of Chinese women, especially of the lower classes, appears

CHAPTER VI

on closer observation even less agreeable than I had thought. The hard fate of so many of the slave-girls, for example, must excite the pity and sympathy of all men and women not altogether selfishly insensible to human sufferings from which they are exempt. But while we have been gazing on a good deal of the darker side of the lives of the women and girls of China, we must not forget that shadows cannot exist without light, so there must be a bright side in life for many Chinese women, and some of the papers read have shown us that no small number of Chinese ladies, independently of European influences, extend noble-minded and practical charity to those amongst their humbler neighbours who may stand in need of such assistance. Possibly some of us may be too apt to judge the better classes of the Chinese by the standards of the lower orders, with whom as a general rule Europeans are chiefly thrown. How would the denizens of our ancient cathedral closes, or the occupants of our manor-houses at home, like foreigners to judge of them by the standard of the inhabitants of the lower stratum of our society and the waifs and strays, who too often in other lands bring the reverse of credit to their country? I cannot help hoping, likewise, that as habit becomes second nature — and that to which we are accustomed seems less dreadful, even when intrinsically as bad — so some things that to us would make existence a purgatory may not be quite so terrible to the women of China as they appear to us. I would fain hope that even in such a matter as foot-binding there may be some alleviation to the sufferings of those who practise it, in the pride that is said to feel no pain. Of the deleterious effects of the practice — physically and mentally — there can be no doubt, and it is most satisfactory to find that the spark of resistance to the fashion of foot-binding has been kindled in many parts of China. As new ideas permeate the empire, I have no doubt the women of China will not be greater slaves to undesirable fashions or customs than are the women of other lands. The greater number of the ills and discomforts of Chinese women, I cannot help thinking, must be eradicated by the people of China themselves; all that outsiders can do is to place the means of doing so within their reach. As year by year the number increases of cultivated and enlightened Chinese ladies, trained in Western science and modes of thought, while retaining their own distinctive characteristics, so will each of them prove a stronger centre from which rays of good influence will reach out to their country-women. I was once given a flower that had rather a remarkable history. I was told that somewhere in Greece a mine had been found that was supposed to have been worked by the ancient Greeks. Its site was marked by great heaps of rocks and refuse. The Greeks of old, great as was their genius, which in some ways exceeded that of modern days, were not acquainted with a great deal that science has revealed to us, and in examining these heaps of stones and rubbish flung out of the mine in days of old, it was found that most of it contained ore, the presence of which had never before been suspected, but which was sufficient in amount to make it worth while submitting the refuse to a process that would extract the latent wealth. So the great heaps of stone were removed, for smelting or some such process, and when they were taken away, from the ground beneath them sprang up plants, which in due time were covered with beautiful small yellow poppies of a kind not previously known to gardeners. It is supposed that the seed of the flowers must have lain hidden in the earth for centuries. May it not be like this with China? In her bosom have long lain dormant the seeds of what we call progress, which have been kept from germinating by the superincumbent weight of ideas, which, while they may contain in themselves some ore worth extracting, must be refined in order to be preserved, and must be uplifted in order to enable the flowers of truth, purity, and happiness to flourish in the land. Two of the heaviest rubbish heaps that crush down the blossom progress are ignorance and prejudice. I trust that the conference just held may prove of use in removing them."

Whatever may be thought of the relative prudence of choosing one's own wife, or having the young lady provided by family diplomacy, as is the Eastern custom, there is no doubt that Chinese women make affectionate wives and mothers. A forlorn woman at Macao, day after day wailing along the shore of the cruel sea that had taken her fisher-husband, waving his coat over the sea, burning incense, and calling upon him unceasingly to return to her, was a mournful sight; and I have seen distracted women passing the clothes of their sick children to and fro over a brisk fire by a running stream, and calling upon the gods they worshipped to circumvent the demons to whose evil action all sickness is attributed. Indeed, the loss of the husband himself would, in the average Chinese opinion, be better for the family than the loss of an only son, as without a male descendant the ancestral worship, on which so much depends for the comfort of the departed members, cannot be carried out in proper form. That the terrors of superstition enter largely into the Chinese mind is clearly shown, but there is also present the saving grace of faith in the possibility of assuaging whatever may be considered the discomforts of the after life, and Chinese are particular in ministering to the wants of the departed. I have seen in Hong Kong two women gravely carrying a small house, tables, chairs, and a horse, all made of tissue paper and light bamboo, to a vacant place where they were reverently burnt, no doubt for the use of a departed husband. This is the same faith that raised the mounds over the Scandinavian heroes, who with their boats or war-horses and their arms were buried beneath them.

When a child is born, a boat made similarly of tissue paper and fixed on a small bundle of straw is launched upon the tide. If it floats away, all will be well; if flung back upon the shore, there is gloom in the house, for Fortune is frowning. Or, when members of the family are lost at sea, similar boats with small figures seated in them, and with squares of gold and silver paper representing money placed at their feet, are sent adrift. Such boats are constantly to be seen floating in the harbour of Hong Kong, each one a sad emblem of poignant sorrow, with that desperate anxiety of those bereft to reach behind the veil that lies in the sub-conscious mind of all humanity.

This is the mournful aspect of Chinese life, especially among the poorer classes. But Chinese ladies, though they take their pleasures in a different manner, are no less actively engaged in the amenities of social intercourse than are their Western sisters. Violent physical exercise does not appeal to them — our compelling muscularity is a hidden mystery to all Eastern people — but visiting among themselves is constant, and the preparation for a visit, the powdering and painting, the hair-dressing, and the careful selection of embroidered costumes, is as absorbing a business as was the preparation of the belles of the court of *Le Roi Soleil*. To the European man the fashion of a Chinese lady's dress seems unchanging — a beautifully embroidered loose jacket, with long pleated skirt and wide trousers, in strong crimson or yellow, or in delicate shades of all colours — but Western women probably know better, as doubtless do the Chinese husbands and fathers, who are usually most generous to the ladies of the family. The general shape is unchanging, for in China it is considered indelicate for a woman to display her figure; but the Chinese milliner is as careful to change the fashion of the embroidery at short intervals as is the French *modiste* to change the form of the robe. Therefore there are always to be procured in the great towns beautiful embroidered costumes in excellent order that have been discarded at the command of tyrant fashion as are the dresses of the fashion-driven ladies of the West.

The etiquette of the preliminaries of a visit is as rigid as is the etiquette of all social intercourse in China; the scarlet visiting card, three or four inches wide and sometimes a foot long — its dimensions being proportioned to the social position of the visitor — being first sent in, and returned with an invitation to enter, while the hostess dons her best attire and meets the visitor at the first, second, or third doorway, according to the rank of the latter, and the elaborate ceremonial on entering the room. These accomplished, the conversation follows the lines that conversation takes where ladies meet ladies all the world over. The friendly pipe is not excluded, and probably books, children, cooks, social incidents, and possibly local politics, form the media of conversation. The social customs of China do not afford much opportunity for scandal; but who can say? Cupid even in China is as ingenious as he is mischievous. Games, too, are indulged in, the Chinese card games being as mysteriously intricate as is their chess.

Should the guest bring her children, the little ones all receive presents, these delicate attentions being never neglected; indeed, the giving of presents at the New Year and other annual festivals is a settled Chinese custom.

CHAPTER VII

Though Hong Kong, when handed over to Great Britain in 1841, was a practically uninhabited island, it has now a population of 377,000, of which 360,000 are Chinese. The city of Victoria is situated round the southern shore of the harbour, and is, next to London, the greatest shipping port in the world. Behind the city steep hills rise to the height of over 1,800 feet, their rugged sides scored by well constructed roads and dotted over with handsome buildings, while a cable tramway leads to the Peak (1,200 feet high), where fine houses and terraces afford in summer accommodation for the European residents, who find in its cool heights relief from the oppressive temperature of the sea level. It is hard to say whether Hong Kong is more beautiful from the harbour or from the Peak. From the one is seen the city crowded round the shore behind the broad praya or sea front, and sweeping up the precipitous sides of the hills — spreading as it climbs from street to terrace, from terrace to villa, up to the very Peak — terrace and villa nestled in the everlasting verdure of the luxuriant tropics, varied by blazes of colour from tree, shrub, and climber, the blue masses of hydrangea at the Peak vying with the brilliant masses of purple bougainvillia, or yellow alamanda of the lower levels, the whole bathed in such sunshine as is rarely seen in temperate regions, while above the blue sky is flecked with light fleecy clouds.

Away to the eastward is the happy valley, a flat oval, around which the hill-sides are devoted to a series of the most beautifully kept cemeteries in the world. Here Christian and Mohammedan, Eastern and Western, rest from their labours, while below them, in the oval valley, every sport and game of England is in full swing.

From the Peak we look down upon the city and the harbour, and our gaze sweeps onward over the flat peninsula of Kowloon to the bare and rugged hills that sweep from east to west. But the interest centres in the magnificent harbour, on whose blue bosom rest the great steamers of every nation trading with the Far East, round whose hulls are flitting the three hundred and fifty launches of which the harbour boasts, whose movements at full speed in a crowded harbour bear witness to the splendid nerve of their Chinese coxswains. Out in the harbour, towards Stonecutter's Island, the tall masts of trim American schooners may be seen, the master — probably part owner — with sometimes his wife on board, and with accommodation aft that the captains of our largest liners might envy, while the thousands of Chinese boats of all descriptions look like swarms of flies moving over the laughing waters of the bay. The hum of the city is inaudible, and even the rasp of the derricks that feed the holds of the steamships or empty them of their cargoes comes up with a softened sound, telling its tale of commercial activity.

At night the scene is still more enchanting, for spread out beneath are gleaming and dancing the thousands of lights afloat and ashore. The outlines of the bay are marked by sweeping curves of light, and the myriad stars that seem to shine more brightly

CHAPTER VII

than elsewhere are mirrored in the dark waters, mingling with the thousands of lights from the boats and shipping.

This is normal Hong Kong, and in the warm season, for in winter it is cold enough to demand the glow of the fire and the cheerful warmth of furs. But the beautiful harbour lashed to wild fury by the dreaded typhoon is a different sight. All may look well to the uninitiated, who wonders to see groups of sampans and lighters, sometimes twenty or more, being towed by single launches to Causeway Bay, the boat harbour of refuge; but the gathering clouds in the south-east, the strong puffy gusts of wind, and the rapidly falling barometer with the characteristic pumping action, warn the watchful meteorological staff that the time has come to hoist the warning signal, while in addition the south-easterly heave of the sea gives notice to the careful sea-captain that he had better not be caught in narrow waters except with both anchors down and a full head of steam ready.

With a blackening sky, increasing wind, and troubled sea there is no longer room for doubt, and active preparations are made ashore and afloat. While cables are lengthened, top hamper made snug, and steam got up on sea, all windows are carefully fastened with hurricane bars on shore, for should a window be blown in when the typhoon is at its height there is no knowing how far the destruction may extend, the walls being sometimes blown out and the contents of the house scattered over the hill-side. I have seen such a typhoon that reached its maximum in the early morning. The whole harbour was foaming with a devil's dance of wild waters, hidden by a thick blanket of spray, through which from time to time great waves were dimly seen dashing over the high wharf premises, or godowns, of Kowloon, while minute-guns of distress boomed from out the wrack of sea and mist, heard as dull thuds in the howling of the mighty typhoon, and calling for help that none could give. By ten o'clock the typhoon had swept on to the north, leaving scores of ships and junks sunk in the harbour, a mile of sampans smashed to pieces at the Kowloon wharves, and hundreds of victims beneath the now moderating seas, while the harbour was filled with floating bales of merchandise.

The incident was the means of demonstrating the organizing capacity of the Chinese. As soon as the sea had moderated sufficiently to allow a launch to live, I sent for a Chinese gentleman and suggested that something should be done to relieve the sufferers and rescue those who still required assistance, and found that already the guild had sent out two powerful launches, one with coffins for the drowned, the other, with a doctor on board, equipped with the necessary means of succour for the injured, and food for those who had lost their all. Steaming along the Kowloon shore an hour afterwards, where the wreckage of boats was heaving and falling in a mass of destruction twenty to thirty feet wide along the sea wall, there was no sign, as might have been expected, of stunned despair; but the crowd of boat-people, men and women, who had escaped with their lives were working with a will and as busy as bees, each endeavouring to save something from the smashed wreckage of what had been their home, the men jumping from one heaving mass to another, diving betimes and struggling with the adverse buffets of fate with an energy none the less for

CHAPTER VII

their stoical acceptance of the inevitable.

Although Hong Kong is a British possession it is essentially a Chinese city. British supervision has seen to it that the streets are wide and all the houses well and solidly built, save a few remaining houses of the era preceding the creation of a sanitary board, and cleanliness of house and surroundings is secured by careful and unremitting inspection. The shops are a mixture of European architecture and Chinese decoration, which runs into rich and elaborate carving and gilding. Outside are hung the same pendant signs that give such colour to the streets of Canton. Blue is the predominant colour worn by all Chinese, save the sweating coolies who toil along the quays of the great port, and the blue crowd that fills the busy streets harmonizes with the surrounding colours. The splendid buildings in what are called the principal streets, where banks, hotels, and counting-houses of the important European firms are situated, with the shops that cater more especially for the wants of foreign residents and tourists, differ but little from the architecture of a European city, while the shops contain all that purchasers can require of European wares, or Chinese and Japanese products wherewith to tempt the inquiring tourist. But the wealthiest part of the city is in the Chinese quarter, and here property has changed hands at startling figures, sometimes at a rate equal to one hundred and sixty thousand pounds an acre. Here the shops are purely Chinese, and every trade may be seen in operation, while the doctor puts up a sign that he cures broken legs, or the dentist displays a small board, from which hang five or six long strings of molars of portentous size showing every phase of dental decay. Everywhere is seen a teeming population instinct with ceaseless activity. Rickshaws rush past, these most convenient little carriages for hire having one coolie in the shafts, while private rickshaws have one or two in addition pushing behind; or the more sedate chair swings by, borne by two or four coolies, the men in front and rear stepping off with different feet so as to prevent the swinging of the chair. The shops in this quarter have abandoned the glass front and are open, save when at night they are closed by planks set up and fastened with a bar behind the last two. The shop is then secure from any attempt to break in from the outside; but cases are on record where armed robbers have slipped in at the last moment and, closing the plank which secured them from observation, produced revolvers and walked off with the contents of the till, leaving the terrified owner and his assistants bound and gagged while they made their escape.

The early life of the city is an interesting study. At five o'clock the people are astir. The working men apparently take their morning meal in the streets, where tables are erected on which are large vessels of rice, and of boiling congee (a mixture of rice flour and water), piles of vegetables of various sorts chopped fine, dishes of scraps of meat, including the uncooked entrails of fowls, pieces of fish, and relishes of soy and other sauces. The hungry customer is handed a bowl half full of rice, on which is placed small portions of the various vegetables and a piece of meat, or some scraps of entrails, over all is poured a ladle full of the boiling congee, and the repast is ready. With his chopsticks the customer, holding the bowl to his wide open mouth, shovels in nearly as much rice as it will hold, then picking from the bowl pieces of the luscious morsels with which it is garnished, he lays them on the yet untouched rice, when he closes his mouth and proceeds with the process of mastication and deglutition. Each mouthful is a course, and the same process is repeated until the morning meal is complete. Hard by may be seen a purveyor of whelks, which are a favourite food, especially with boys, who have all the excitement of gambling in satisfying their hunger. The whelks are in a basket, to the handle of which a dozen pieces of wire with crooked ends are attached by long cords. A small boy appears and lays a cash upon the stall, at the same time drawing from a deep bamboo joint a bamboo slip, one of the many in the pot. At the end of the slip is a number, or a blank, and the hungry lover of chance may find the result of his first venture a blank, or he may be fortunate enough to draw a prize with a number, which represents the number of whelks that he is to receive. These he deftly picks out with one of the crooked wires. They must, of course, be consumed "on the premises," for the cautious caterer takes no chances by permitting the wire to be detached from the cord. Boys are active and unscrupulous, and crooked wires cost money. Balls of rice flour, fried in lard, are another favourite food of the streets, and sweetmeats of appalling stickiness and questionable preparation are always to be found in Chinese quarters. The morning crowd is always good-humoured, chaffing and laughing with a heartiness that explodes the European idea of Chinese stolidity and want of expression.

The Chinese workman eats but twice a day. His morning meal is between six and eight o'clock, and his afternoon meal is at four.

By this time the boats have arrived from Kowloon with their loads of vegetables, and the small hawkers are busily carrying them from house to house for the consumption of Chinese households, while the outlying greengrocers are being supplied with their daily stock, in the setting out of which great care is exercised, the Chinese greengrocer having an artistic eye for effect. No small shop does a more flourishing business than the druggist's and herbalist's, the Chinese having faith in the use of "simples," though remedies including the calcined teeth of tigers and vertebræ of serpents are not without their moral effect, and the mystery of a pill three-quarters of an inch in diameter has yet to be fathomed. At the Chinese New Year, tied up over every door will be seen a small bundle of vegetables, consisting of five plants: the *Acorus calamus*, representing a sword, and the *Euphorbia*, a fighting-iron, to ward off evil spirits; the onion, to guard against the spirit of malaria; the *Artemisia vulgaris* and the *Davallia tennifolia*. This charm is as efficacious as the house leek that, in the imaginative pre-national school days, was carefully planted on the roof of Irish cottages as a sure preservative against fire.

But the busiest man in the early morning is the barber, for the Chinese workman does not shave his own head, and small crowds assemble in each barber's shop, where tongues wag freely, and some read the morning papers while awaiting their turn. However great the crowd, there is no sign of hurry in the manipulation of the placid barber. Not alone is the front of the head shaved, but the eyebrows and eyelashes are attended to; then the ears are explored and cleaned with minute care; and, lastly, the client is massaged and shampooed while he sits bent forward, the hammering upon back and sides being by no means gentle, and ending with a resounding smack with the hollowed palm of the barber's hand. The constant manipulation of the ears is supposed to be injurious as tending to produce deafness, but without it the customer would not consider that he had value for his thirty cash, the usual fee — about one-third of a cent. The end of the operation is the plaiting of the long queue, which between the real and the false hair freely used reaches nearly to the heels, and is finished by a silk tassel plaited into the end. Sometimes a man may be seen plaiting his own queue, which he does by taking it over the rung of a ladder, and moving backwards so as to preserve the strain.

Among the skilled workmen, the sawyer and the stonecutter are most in evidence to the ordinary visitor, who is astonished to see a squared log two feet in diameter being sawn by a single man. Having got the log into position, one man with a frame-saw does the whole business. He stands on top, and the work is extremely arduous; but an enormous amount of timber is sawn in this way. The stonecutter has a lighter job. The Chinese are very expert quarrymen, and cut out by iron or wooden wedges great blocks of granite, the wedge-holes having been prepared by iron chisel-headed bolts. Wooden wedges are then driven in and wetted, the expansion of the wedge forcing out the block, which requires but little squaring, so carefully is the cleavage effected.

One generic difference between the physical formation of Western and Eastern races is the facility with which the latter can sit upon their heels. An Asiatic will sink down upon his heels with as much ease and with as restful comfort as can a European upon a chair; and in stonecutting the workman may be seen sitting upon the stone on which he is working, sometimes seated on the edge while chiselling the perpendicular side below him. In this position a row of workmen look at a distance like a row of vultures sitting upon a ledge.

The lowest form of labour in Hong Kong is the work of the coolies, who carry coals and building materials to the Peak district; and here we have a striking evidence of the patient industry and extraordinary ingenuity with which the piece-work labourer secures the largest possible amount of result from the day's labour. Up the steep hill-side every brick or basket of sand and lime that has gone to build the houses and barracks of the Peak district has been carried up in the double baskets, suspended from the bamboo carrying-pole of a working coolie, who is paid by the load. Now a heavy load, sometimes weighing a hundredweight, carried up very steep roads for two miles or so, means slow progress, with many rests. The coolie manages to reduce the intervals of rest to the smallest compass. Placing two loads together, he carries one for fifty yards and there deposits it, returning for the second, which is carried up one hundred yards. Dropping that, he — or she, for the matter of that, for the coolie hill-carriers are sometimes women, not seldom old and feeble — returns to the first load and carries the burden fifty yards beyond the second, which is in turn taken up in the same way. There is no standing idle or sitting down to rest, the only relief being that of dropping the load and walking back down hill to take up the one left behind. This system of overlapping saves

CHAPTER VII

all the time that otherwise must be lost in resting, as no human being could carry up a load to the Peak without frequent intervals of rest.

After the day's work is ended the workman does not affect a tavern. He dearly loves a game, or, more strictly speaking, a gamble; and while all gambling-houses are put down with a strong hand, no conceivable official ingenuity could circumvent the gambling propensities of a people whose instruments of games of chance are not confined to cards or dice. The number of seeds in a melon, or any other wager on peculiarities of natural objects will do as well, and afford no damning evidence should an officious member of the police force appear. The game of chi-mooe is not confined to the working people, but is a favourite game with all classes, and the shouts and laughter that accompany it now and again bring complaints from the neighbours whose rest is disturbed. The game is simple and is played by two. One suddenly flings out his hand with one, two, or more fingers extended, at the same moment the other must guess the number. Curling has been called the roaring game, but no curler ever made a greater racket than two excited chi-mooe players. One would imagine that the guessing of the number of fingers extended must be a matter of pure chance, but a Chinese gentleman assured me that in the flinging forward of the hand there is a muscular difference in the form if one, two, three, or more fingers are to be extended, and this difference is observed with lightning rapidity by an expert player.

However content the adult Chinaman may be with sedentary

amusements, the energy of youth is in full force in the Chinese schoolboy. He is rapidly acquiring a taste for European games, such as cricket and football, but he has always played the game of hopscotch, but little differing from the game played in an English village. Where a ring can be formed he also plays a game of shuttlecock, the only instrument being a cork or piece of light wood with two or three feathers to regulate its flight and fall. This is played solely with the feet, the shuttlecock being kicked from one to the other with extraordinary dexterity. The shuttlecock is often kept up for five or even ten minutes at a time, foot and eye working together with wonderful precision.

CHAPTER VIII

There is one sport in which the adult Chinaman shines. Each year in the month of June the boatmen and fishermen hold a festival at which the great feature is the dragon-boat races. The dragon-boat is about ninety feet long and only wide enough to admit of two men with paddles sitting side by side on each thwart. In this boat from sixty to eighty men are seated, while in the centre stands a man with a drum or gong before him on which he beats the time. A man stands at the stern with a long steering paddle, and a boy sits in front with two lines in his hands attached to a large dragon's head with which the bow is adorned, and which moves from side to side as the lines are pulled. Two contending boats paddle to the starting-buoy and at a signal they are off. The frantic encouragement of the men beating time, the furious but rhythmic splash of nearly two hundred paddles in the onrushing boats, and the natural movement from side to side of the brightly coloured dragons' heads, is one of the finest and most inspiring sights imaginable. Every muscle is strained, and no sport on earth shows for the time a more tremendous effort of muscular energy. Sometimes in the excitement of the race the boats collide, in which event the race must be run again, for the mixture of paddles makes it impossible to disentangle without a dead stop. But such a *contretemps* leads to no mischief or quarrelling. The accident is treated good-humouredly all round, and it only means another race. On the river at Canton literally thousands of boats make a line to see the races paddled. There are no police and no stewards of the course, but no boat ever attempts to break the line or cause any obstruction.

The Chinese delight in festivals and spectacular effects, in which they give proof of organizing capacity. A very striking festival was that in honour of a son of the god of war, held at Macao every tenth year in the intercalary moon. It was a guild procession — watchmakers, tailors, shoemakers, etc. Each guild had carried before it a great triangular, richly embroidered banner, also an umbrella of honour. Many had also a long piece of embroidery carried horizontally on poles. There were ornamental chairs of the usual type, some with offerings to the gods, some with wooden drums. Each guild had its band; some string bands, some reeds and gongs, some Chinese viols and mandolins, the latter being frequently played while held over the head or resting on the back of the neck. Each guild marched two and two behind the band, the members being dressed in mauve silk coats and broad red or yellow sash tied round the waist with richly embroidered ends down each leg. The watchmakers' guild all carried watches on the right breast. Children, richly dressed in medieval costume, were mounted on caparisoned ponies, and some guilds had cars on which were allegorical groups of children. In some cases, by an ingenious arrangement of an iron frame, a child held a sword at length which, apparently, pierced another child through back and breast. The variety of these groups was very great. From time to time the procession stopped, and then the children were taken down for a rest, the iron frames being disconnected from their easily detachable sockets. In the meantime each group was attended by men who held umbrellas over the children to protect them from the sun.

Each guild had its attendant coolies carrying stools, and when the procession stopped the members at once sat down, starting up at once on the sound of a gong that regulated the halting and starting, when the stools were taken up by the coolies.

The procession finished with a dragon carried by twenty-six men. It was a hundred and forty feet long, the back of green and silver scales, the sides being stripes of red, green, pink, and yellow silk. This dragon was preceded by a man, who danced before it with a large ball representing the moon. At this the dragon made dashes from one side of the street to the other, but was staved off by another, who carried a ball surrounded by gilt rays. This probably represented the sun saving the moon from being swallowed by the dragon, as is supposed to take place in an eclipse. The dragon went along the street with sinuous rushes from side to side. Where there was room it wound round and round, but uncoiled on the touch upon its tail of the gilt ball with the golden rays. The procession took an hour and a half to pass a given point. The most perfect order prevailed, the crowd keeping a clear space. At the finish each guild went to its own district, and the decorations were carefully stowed away for future use.

Such a festival is, of course, a local holiday; but the only legal Chinese holidays are at the New Year, when all business is suspended. The viceroy puts his seal away; the governor and the magistrate follow suit; the merchant closes his place of business and squares his books, while his employees take the opportunity to revisit their homes in the country. The shopkeeper generally has a feast for all his people, at the conclusion of which he makes a speech, wishing each and all a "Happy New Year," in certain cases adding, "and I hope that you, and you," mentioning the names, "will obtain good situations." This is a delicate intimation to the persons named that their services are dispensed with. In ordinary Chinese business affairs all accounts are closed and balanced and all debts paid at the New Year.

In Hong Kong the cessation from business lasts for ten days. At this time booths are erected on either side of several streets in the Chinese quarter, on which are displayed everything that appeals to the fancy of the crowds with which the streets are thronged day and night. There is an enormous sale of a white bell-shaped flower, something like a large erica, known as the New Year flower; goldfish in glass globes are a favourite purchase, and on the stalls rigged up under cover are thousands of articles to suit the fancy of all classes. The heterogeneous stocks-in-trade are evidently got together by roving pedlars or collectors, who find their annual harvest at New Year. Here may be purchased everything, from a piece of bronze or porcelain to a small clay figure, of which a dozen may be bought for a couple of cents. Sometimes an article of real value may be picked up by a seeker after second-hand chances, while eager children spend their cents in smaller investments; but the annual bazaar has one peculiarity that speaks well for the masses of the Chinese people. In all the thousands of articles and pictures exhibited for sale there is not to be seen the slightest indication of even a suspicion of immodesty.

Over every door is now found a small ornament of peacock's feathers, that being a lucky emblem. The social ceremonies are many and elaborate. New Year visits of congratulation are paid; the family graves are visited, and due honours paid to the dead; and presents are offered and accepted. During the holidays immense quantities of fire-crackers are exploded, a string costing many dollars being sometimes hung from an upper balcony, the explosion of the crackers, with loud sounding bombs at intervals, lasting for several minutes, and filling the street with apparently the sharp crackle of musketry and the boom of heavy guns. At the end of the festival the streets are filled with the vermilion paper that covered the exploded fireworks.

Next to the New Year's fair, the most interesting study in Hong Kong was the crowds who came down from Canton and the outlying districts of Kwangtung province for the annual race-meeting — a European institution that flourishes at every coast port in China, the horses being hardy little Mongolian ponies, and the sport excellent. During the three days' racing it was the custom practically to allow a Saturnalia, and the police closed their eyes to offences against the gambling laws, only pouncing upon faked pu-chee boxes, loaded dice, or other unfair instruments of gambling. On the race-course these gamblers plied their trade between the races, and afforded an opportunity of seeing the most diverse and curious games of chance and skill. One game I do not remember to have seen elsewhere. Round a flat stone was drawn a circle with a diameter of about five feet, divided into spaces radiating from centre to circumference. On the stone the proprietor placed a heap of copper coin. The players placed their stakes in any division chosen; then the proprietor placed a weight on his head, from which he jerked it at a distance of about twelve feet. If the weight hit the heap of coin he took the stakes, but if it fell on one of the divisions, the player who staked on that division took the heap of coin on the stone.

Again, on a board was painted a number of Chinese characters, on any one of which the players placed their stakes. The proprietor then handed a bag to a player, who took out a handful of disks, like draughtsmen, on each of which was a character. The handful was placed on the table and sorted, each character being placed on the corresponding character on the board. The player received as many times his stakes as there were characters drawn corresponding to that on which he had placed his money. If no corresponding character was drawn, then he lost.

In pursuance of a determined effort to stop the ravages of plague, the custom of winking at what were undoubtedly irregularities was abandoned, so as to check the influx of the many thousands of "sporting" vermin to Hong Kong at race time, and once stopped the custom could not be permitted to again establish itself.

It must not be assumed that all the interests of Hong Kong are exhausted by a cursory or even a lengthened examination of its streets and outdoor amusements. Hong Kong boasts of excellent schools, the Queen's College and St. Joseph's Schools being the largest. There is an excellent boarding-school for the sons and daughters of Chinese gentlemen, where the utmost care is exercised in the supervision of the pupils; a medical college exists in which the entire course of medical education can be taken; and it is now proposed to establish a university that may yet be the centre of higher education for Chinese students.

The charities of China are not sufficiently realized; but while there is no general organization of charitable societies, as in European countries, individual charity is widespread. The poor receive gifts of clothing in winter; in times of famine or of scarcity rice is often distributed free, or sold under cost price, or coffins are supplied to the poor. In Hong Kong the Chinese community have built a well equipped hospital for general patients, and also a plague hospital for the reception of the victims of this scourge that has annually visited the city for the past fifteen years.

There is also in connection with the "Tung Wa" hospital an institution called the Pow-li-un-kok, where orphan children are taken, as are also received the children who from time to time are rescued by the police from harpies who are carrying them through Hong Kong for the purpose of selling them as domestic slaves. These children are brought up, and the boys placed in situations where they can earn their living, while arrangements are made for the marriage of the girls when they reach a marriageable age. Chinese frequently take girls from the institution as wives. It is also used as a rescue home for fallen and friendless girls for whom also husbands are often found.

These are but brief sketches of phases of Chinese life as it presents itself to one who has had no opportunity for the study of cause and effect that would require long years of careful observation. We know but little of the real China. The average European, if he thinks of China at all, sets her down as a nation just emerging from barbarism, untruthful, deceitful, and having more than her share of original sin. On the other hand, the Chinese who have come in contact with foreign Powers regard them as bullies, who have by their destructive prowess forced themselves upon the Middle Kingdom and deprived the Emperor and his government of their sovereignty over the various concessions at the treaty ports. No definite complaint has been formulated on this matter so far; but it must not be assumed that there is no feeling of irritation on the subject in the minds of many of the educated Chinese. The phenomenal successes of Japan in war, and the rapidity with which she has compelled her acceptance on terms of equality by foreign nations, has set the Chinese a-thinking, and we know not how soon the demand for reconsideration of foreign relations may become inconveniently pressing.

The death of the late Dowager-Empress and of the young Emperor, whose sudden and mysterious death was the crowning tragedy of years of sorrow and restraint, has placed upon the Imperial throne an infant whose father (the Regent) is a prince of enlightened and progressive views. Already great changes have been made, and greater still are projected. The isolation of centuries is being modified, and in nearly three thousand schools in China the English language is being taught, and Western methods of instruction are being introduced. Many internal reforms are being considered, and the principle of the training to arms of all young men has been decided upon. If we take even one-tenth of the population as being liable to military training, it would give a crop of recruits of forty millions! It remains to be seen if such an evidence of power will set in motion the military instinct, or if a different system of education may not result in a demand for drastic changes in the whole system and constitution of government. There is in the Southern Provinces a strong leaven of opinion formed by students who have been trained in the colleges of the United States. Their aspirations are mainly on Republican lines; but I do not find that this solution commends itself to the people of the Northern Provinces.

The establishment of local councils has been decided upon, the inevitable result of which will be the lessening of the autocratic power of provincial officials. Whether the change will result in the increase of efficiency or the decrease of corruption time alone will tell; but we may rest assured that however loudly reformers may demand changes of system and custom, the present generation will be very slow to move. When the Chinese people do move the advance will be probably steady, and will certainly be maintained. Should a military instinct be evolved, an alliance with Japan might at a future period form the strongest combination in the world, and when that time arrives the present system of extra-territoriality of the concessions, so convenient for foreigners, will go by the board.

At present, however, China offers in her markets an object for the keen competition of the manufacturing nations of the world, in which the British manufacturer bids fair to be beaten, especially by our friends in Germany, whose watchword in commerce, as in everything besides, is "thorough."

The awakening of China means her entrance into strong competition for her full share of the trade of the world. With her great commercial capacity and enormous productive power she will be able to a large extent to supply her own wants, and will certainly reach out to distant foreign markets. Exploration discloses the fact that in bygone ages Chinese influence has reached to the uttermost parts of the globe. It is to be found in the ornaments of the now extinct Beothuks of Newfoundland, and in the buried pottery of the Incas of Peru, while in Ireland a number of Chinese porcelain seals have been discovered at different times and in some cases at great depths, the period, judging from the characters engraved upon them, being about the ninth century A.D. It may be that with the increase of commercial activity, wages will rise to such an extent as to bring the cost of production in China to the level of that of other nations; if not, then the future competition may produce results for the wage-earners of Liverpool, Birmingham, and Manchester evoking bitter regret that the policy of coaxing, worrying, bullying, and battering the Far Eastern giant into the path of commercial energy has been so successful. Given machinery, cheap labour, unsurpassed mineral deposits, and educated determination to use them, and China will prove a competitor before whom all but the strongest may quail.

The only competition for which she will never enter is a competition in idleness. Every man works to the full extent of his capacity, and the virile vigour of the nation is intact.

With the coming change in her educational system that will strike off the fetters of competitive memorizing and substitute rational reflection, China must be a potent factor in the affairs of the world. When that time comes let us hope that the relations between China and the British Empire will be the outcome of mutual confidence and goodwill.

图书在版编目（CIP）数据

遇见中国：卜力眼中的东方世界／（英）亨利·阿瑟·卜力著；李菲译.—上海：上海社会科学院出版社，2017
ISBN 978-7-5520-2076-2

Ⅰ.①遇… Ⅱ.①亨… ②李… Ⅲ.①中国历史－史料－1898－1903 Ⅳ.①K250.6

中国版本图书馆CIP数据核字（2017）第174901号

遇见中国——卜力眼中的东方世界

著　　者：［英］亨利·阿瑟·卜力
译　　者：李　菲
责任编辑：孙　洁
封面设计：周清华
出版发行：上海社会科学院出版社
　　　　　上海顺昌路622号　邮编200025
　　　　　电话总机021-63315900　销售热线021-53063735
　　　　　http://www.sassp.org.cn　E-mail: sassp@sass.org.cn
排　　版：南京展望文化发展有限公司
印　　刷：上海盛通时代印刷有限公司
开　　本：890×1240　1/32开
印　　张：8
插　　页：10
字　　数：168千字
版　　次：2017年11月第1版　2018年4月第2次印刷

ISBN 978-7-5520-2076-2/K·404　　　　　定价：48.00元

版权所有　翻印必究